Training
Your Children
to Handle
Money

Malcolm D. MacGregor

Training Your Children to Handle Money

Malcolm MacGregor

Reality Ministries, Inc.

P.O. BOX 5926

SAN JOSE, CA 95150

Published by Reality Ministries, Inc.
P.O. Box 5926, San Jose, California 95150

Printed in the United States of America

Library of Congress Cataloging in Publication Data

MacGregor, Malcolm, 1945-
  Training your children to handle money.

  1. Finance, Personal—Study and teaching. I. Title.
HG179.M229   332.024'007   80-17579
ISBN 0-87123-540-4

Dedication

To my children, Greg, George and Margaret Mary, who suffered the training to provide material for this book and now, Gordon, who will have to live under the shadow of this book.

To my wife who has so much patience with a thick-headed husband. Her support is priceless.

To my father who has always said he taught me everything I know—not everything he knows, just everything I know!

And, finally, to my mother, without whose son this book would have never been completed.

Preface

There are all sorts of theories when it comes to child-rearing and training. Rather than get hung up on the differences we have, I would like to ask you to read through these chapters and accept the approaches I have here as the best that I have been able to come up with in working with my three children. I will attempt to show you what seems to have worked with our children and those children I am familiar with who are in our close circle of friendship. I don't claim to have exhausted all the personality types and problems that would have come up. I have done the best job that I know how to search out scriptures to find out what kind of attitudes and approaches God commends toward our money and how those apply to the training of children. I recognize that there are going to be certain areas of my own prejudice that are bound to come through in the writing, so don't throw the book away because you disagree with one paragraph. Instead, put the disagreement aside and see if maybe, by the time you finish the whole book, it doesn't make sense, at least for some children.

A final clarification. I refer from time to time to my three children and other times to my three oldest children. The writing of this manuscript covered about 24 months. Our fourth child was born during the 22nd month.

Contents

PART I

Facing Up to Your Responsibility

1

WHAT??!! Me Teach Money Management?!?

Just as you stuff this evening's meatloaf into the baking pan, your little Suzy dashes into the kitchen. "Let's go out to dinner tonight, Mom," she proposes gleefully.

"Oh, honey, that would be nice," you sigh, "but we just don't have the money in the budget this week."

Undaunted, she replies, "Why don't you just write a check?"

Your wife and young son squeeze through the door, laden with packages. "Honey," she chimes, "look at all these sheets and towels I got on sale at the department store."

You groan inside, "Oh, sweetheart, I thought we had agreed that we just weren't going to spend more money this month."

"That's okay," your son confidently assures you. "Mommy didn't spend any money. She just charged it!"

You *are* training your child in money matters. Your child is learning very subtly how to manage his money and make choices by observing the way you manage *your* money and make *your* choices. Problems in handling money are the root cause of about two-thirds of the divorces in this country, so it's obvious to me that most parents have failed spectacularly in preparing their children for handling money in the real world.

Many a young couple has sat in front of my desk, ready for the divorce court, blaming each other for their financial incompetence. It shouldn't have happened. Here's how it sometimes develops: The young husband was from a family that tried to prepare him in all areas of life. However, their attitude was that since he was one of the family, there were certain things he would do as part of the family—without pay—and his needs would be taken care of.

He went through high school, then on to college where his tuition and other costs were paid by Mom and Dad. They also sent him $35-$50 a month in spending money. In his senior year, he met the "girl of his dreams."

The young woman came from a fine Christian family that had sent her to the same Christian college. She too was not paid for any of the chores she performed around the house; rather, her parents shared the attitude that they would simply take care of her needs. Her college fees were paid and she received a monthly living allowance with, of course, some of the little extras that she was able to wheedle out of Dad when she went home for vacations.

This couple euphorically approached the altar, pronounced their "I do's," and were swept into wedded bliss and a life of happiness. Right? Most likely, *wrong*. If this couple had been properly trained to handle money, their marriage might have had a chance to work; but they had received no training. They will probably go out and establish their married life based on the financial misunderstandings that they developed as children, watching their parents.

The Bible is the best guidebook for teaching your children—even about money. In Proverbs 24:3, 4 we read, "Any enterprise is built by wise planning, becomes strong through common sense, and profits wonderfully by keeping abreast of the facts" (TLB). This verse lists the three essential elements of any good system: planning, control, and feedback. If you are going to be successful at anything, you must first plan: set goals that are stepping-stones toward the objectives you have established for your life. Second, you must control the situation, which is the actual process of keeping records and measuring whether or not you are going to reach those goals. Third, watch the feedback, the method for evaluating. Is the goal reasonable? Should I change the goal?

You must train your child to make plans, to make choices regarding those plans, and to have procedures to evaluate whether or not he is on target in reaching his goals.

God promises that if you "train up a child in the way he should go, even when he is old he will not depart from it" (Prov. 22:6, NASB). Recognize that if your child is to attain financial freedom, he will be successful because you trained him how to obtain that freedom. Your child's success, or failure, in life can depend to a large degree on what you, his parents, teach him.

At this point, most of you are probably thinking, *Oh wow, how can I teach my kids financial freedom when my checkbook is a national disaster? Me teaching my children how to handle money would be like Phyllis Diller teaching in a charm school!*

Maybe the apostle Paul was writing to people with a similar problem, when he asked, "You, therefore, who teach another, do you not teach yourself?" (Rom. 2:21, NASB). *You can do it.* In high school I played on the junior varsity basketball team and under a man who had never coached basketball before. In fact, he stood about 5'4", so he had never really *played* basketball before; but he did an outstanding job teaching us the fundamentals of basketball—how to move, pass, and position ourselves. We did well that year, winning all but one or two games.

Toward the end of the season, I asked the coach how he was able to teach us since he had never played. He explained that he had a couple of books on basketball theory and a file on teaching basketball. He just tried to stay a day ahead of the team.

I was very impressed with that. He didn't know everything about basketball, but he was willing to learn, one day at a time, and thus be prepared to teach us new fundamentals each day.

Therefore, don't worry because your finances are out of control. Instead, just make sure you're one lesson ahead of your child. As you begin to apply sound principles in your own life, you will find it easy to teach your child. The fact that you have purposed to teach your child to attain financial freedom is one of the most important steps in attaining your own financial freedom.

You may not agree with everything I say, but the guidelines I give in this book do come from experience. The principles have worked, not only for my children, but for children of my close friends. There may be some children who are exceptions, but the principles are consistent with Scripture, so make a determined effort to teach them, and you will raise a money-wise child.

Teaching money matters to children is not easy, but your struggles will be rewarded. One of God's key principles is, "He who is faithful in a very little thing is faithful also in much" (Luke 10:10a, NASB). If you teach your child to handle the dimes he gets in his early years, he *is* going to be able to handle the thousands he earns as an adult.

2

Roads to Ruin

"We Can't Afford It"

The statement "We can't afford it" is probably the shoddiest excuse you can give to your child for not providing something for him. What you imply is, "God is not doing a very good job taking care of us, so we can't take care of you in that area."

If "can't afford" is the only reason you are saying no to a child's request, then I believe you ought to find a way to afford it. That doesn't mean you're going out to buy everything your child wants. It just means you are going to work with him to reach his goal.

If there is something *you* really want, that you strongly desire (e.g., a car, a home, a vacation), you and your spouse are willing to sacrifice many things to attain that goal. If a child really wants something, I think you ought to allow him to make a plan and see what he will have to pay to obtain it. If, indeed, his desire is for something that is worthwhile and affordable, then he will be willing to work for it.

In my book *Your Money Matters*, I related the story of when my two oldest boys came running in, wanting to buy bikes. At that point in my life, very frankly, I did not have the money to just go out and buy bikes for them. But I began to speculate as to why the boys were asking about bikes. I soon discovered that their neighbor friends had all gotten bikes. My boys and their sister shared one bicycle; and it was an old one.

So I began to ask myself, "Do they know how to ride a bike?"

Well, yes, they know how to ride a bike.

"Will they ride carefully?"

Yes, they have learned the safety rules and would be careful.

"Will they take good care of a bike?"

No. One thing they had demonstrated was their total lack of consideration in taking care of that bike we had provided for them. They parked it behind the car a couple of times, it was left out in the rain, and it was not maintained carefully.

So I looked at the boys and said, "Okay, guys, we can buy your bikes."

"Yay!"

"But wait a second. This is what we'll do. You each save your money, and for every dollar you save, I'll match it with a dollar. And when we have enough money between the two of us for that bike, we'll go out and buy it."

Well, that started the big plan. The boys began saving their money and I began matching. Greg, my oldest son, acquired a paper route and finally saved enough money for half of his bike, so we sat down and looked through the "Thrifties," and the advertisements in the newspapers, to find a used ten-speed bike. We went out and looked at a couple, and found one that was in good condition, for the money we had, leaving some for repairs since it did need a little work.

We bought the bicycle on a Monday evening, so I took it with me to work on Tuesday and dropped it off at the bike shop. I would pick it up Wednesday.

Wednesday was my counseling night at the church, so I did not come home for dinner. I finally arrived home about 10:30 that evening. As I walked in the door, there was a chair in the middle of the living room with a note in Greg's handwriting attached, saying, "Dad, bring the bike in the house and I will take care of it in the morning."

That bike has never been left out in the rain, never been parked behind the car, and if it's not being used, is normally locked carefully in the garage; and Greg keeps it in top-notch shape. Because I was willing to work with him toward his dream, he was then able to learn responsibility in taking care of that bike.

My second son, George, began saving his money for the bike that he wanted. About a year later, shortly after Greg had purchased his bike, we moved to a new home that included three acres of land. George decided he wanted a mini-bike.

Well, I wasn't terribly excited about that, but I thought, *Will he be careful with it? Will he manage it? Will it teach him some skills—how to maintain and repair motors?* I felt that this could be a good thing.

So I said, "Okay, George, let's establish two rules before we go any further. Number one, no one will be allowed to use the mini-bike without our permission. You must have either my permission or Mom's permission to be able to use it, and certainly no neighborhood kids will be allowed to use it unless we have okayed it.

"And number two, the bike will never be ridden off our property. If you violate the first rule, I'll restrict the use of the bike for three months. If you violate the second rule, then I'll confiscate the mini-bike and sell it immediately. Now, under those restrictions, knowing that you can ride it only on our property, and no one can ride it without our permission, is it something you still want?"

"Yeah, Dad, I just gotta have it," he insisted.

Well, we finally had enough money between us to buy the mini-bike; but George decided he would much rather buy a ten-speed, because he knew he would be able to ride that to the local grocery store and take it to school. You see, I allowed him to go through a period of saving and planning to arrive at a mature conclusion. I didn't impose my opinion on him. I advised him that a ten-speed would be a wiser investment, but if he wanted to buy a mini-bike, we would work for it.

Even though we couldn't afford the bikes, my wife and I were willing to work with the boys toward their dreams, and, through the process, helped them each learn valuable lessons in self-denial (there were many short-term pleasures given up while saving the money), planning, and decision-making.

My boys learned that dreams are not fulfilled overnight, but that an "enterprise built by wise planning" (they had to figure out ways to earn the money) "becomes strong through common sense" (George learned that the mini-bike was not the best for him at that time), "and profits wonderfully by keeping abreast of facts" (each had a savings account and kept track of local prices for bikes).

Let me make certain that you understand me in this matter. There are many things you will *not buy* for your child. Buying a horse, if you live in Manhattan, would not be the wisest investment. But, if your child wants that horse more than anything in the world, can't you work toward that dream?

Have him investigate the initial cost of the horse.

Where would the horse be kept? Let him find out about zoning laws. Let him talk to a stable owner about the impossibility of keeping a horse in a garage.

How much does it cost to maintain a horse at a stable? How many times a week would he have to take care of the horse? How much will the commuting cost?

Let him know that the family budget has priority items (food, rent, car, etc.) and you can allocate only $5.00 per month of the family budget toward keeping a horse.

How is he proposing to earn the rest? Suppose he is willing to fast one day a week. Would you be willing to give him the $2.50 you would have spent on his food?

Do you recognize the possibilities? Rather than saying, "We can't afford it," you can help your child learn the costs of his wants and desires. You can also help him come to mature decisions about these wants and desires. Finally, you can teach him to make sacrifices toward his dream, leaving room for a great God to meet the desires of his heart.

Money—The Love Substitute

Too often I see a father trying to buy his family's affection with money, rather than spending a little love. One such man I knew was very successful, with earnings in the upper 10 percent income bracket. He achieved this by starting his own business, working 12 to 14 hours a day for six and seven days a week.

When he and his wife came to me for counseling, their 17-year-old son was in jail on a drug charge, and their 16-year-old daughter had just announced that she was pregnant.

This couple had given each of their children tennis lessons, piano lessons, memberships in all the right clubs, cars when they turned 16—"everything that we never had when we were kids. *What happened?*"

They didn't give their children *love*; that's what happened. Finding time to spend with the children is a problem with every parent in this busy society. Feeling guilty, the parents in the above case bought things as substitutes for the attention they should have given their kids. Actually, all they had to do was talk to them.

My schedule is about as full as anyone's—maybe more than most. And frankly, I'm not that good of a father. The thing that I do, however, is talk to the kids about it. On a regular basis, I sit down and ask them how I'm doing. I express to them the frustrations I feel with my work, and ask them to pray for me. I also ask them to inform me when I'm becoming "distant" from them.

As each of my children turns thirteen, I give him a cassette tape containing a personal message to him. One of the things I tell him is that I have a tendency to get involved in everything under the sun, except him—not by design, but just because that's the type of person I am. I want him to know that I'm committed to his success, and that he needs to help me keep that commitment.

On the tape I also tell him that if he ever needs me, and I seem to be distant and not meeting his needs, all he needs to do is hand me the tape and I'll know what he means. I promise him I will drop whatever I'm doing and try to meet the need he is expressing. So far, I've not had any of the kids feel so neglected that he had to lay his tape in front of me.

It's not necessarily the amount of time that you spend *with* your child that is important. Many parents are "with" their children a lot, but never get involved in their lives. The parent who really needs to examine his priorities is the one who arrives home from work, sits down in front of the TV and doesn't speak to anyone the whole evening. This parent's "absence" is most destructive.

If you find yourself frequently reaching into your wallet to send your child skating, to the show, or out shopping, ask yourself if it wouldn't be better to give him some time—not more money.

The Word "No"

"No" is one word I would like to remove from your vocabulary when dealing with your child. Now, that doesn't mean you should give your child everything he asks for, but it means you never say no without a reason. If the answer is really no, you should find a way to help your child to come up with that answer.

I was working at my desk one morning when one of the boys came in and exclaimed, "Hey, Dad, ARPTZB-AFTZVVYT-RYTUBXYZ-TTRUPUZVVY-QTR-OBTRFWURT!" Now, if that sentence looks like gibberish to you, then you understand what I heard. I really didn't hear what my son said. But I turned to him and said, "No." That's the age-old parent's "out." When in doubt, say no. You can't get into trouble by saying no—can you?

As my son turned to walk out of the room, I stopped him and confessed, "Son, wait a second; I wasn't really listening to what you had to say. Will you forgive me?"

He looked at me and said, "Sure, Dad."

"Ask me again—please?"

"Dad, is it okay if we go roller skating this afternoon?"

I thought about it. I hadn't done anything with my family that week (I really try to do something with them every week), and hadn't roller skated in a long time. I would be finished with my work by then, and it sounded like a fun family outing. I said, "Okay."

Initially, I wasn't even listening to my son. I was so preoccupied with my work and my own importance that I neglected the importance God wants me to place on my children. I'm responsible to train them and to bring them up properly. If I get more preoccupied with *my* interests than *their* interests, I'm doing them a disservice.

When I take the word "no" out of my vocabulary, I've forced

myself to listen to what my kids say to me. But I'm not stuck with saying yes to everything they ask; I just try not to say no. This is possible only by planning ahead, by educating them well enough so they can come up with an answer themselves. If they're unable yet to make such a decision, I use the situation as an opportunity to instruct them.

For a number of dietary reasons, our family no longer eats candy and heavy sugar items. If one of the children asks permission to buy candy at the store, I don't say no. I simply ask him what the family rules are. We, as a family, discussed this dietary restriction and the children know our reasons and are in *partial* agreement. (Can you ever get complete agreement when so many friends are eating candy?) They answer their own question with "no."

While living in Hawaii, we discovered that fireworks were legal there at certain times of the year. This precipitated immediate requests for the purchase and use of firecrackers and bottle rockets. The obvious answer was no, but I refused to just say that, so an instruction time ensued.

After I explained the dangers of such fireworks, Greg answered his original question with another question. "Well, we probably shouldn't use them alone, but can't you buy them and be with us when we shoot them off?"

This seemed to be a reasonable request and so we proceeded to do just that—at no personal sacrifice, since I probably enjoy fireworks more than they do!

Do you see what I'm doing? I'm teaching my children to think through their requests in light of instruction given to them. As they ask a question that has a "no" answer, I respond according to whether I've given them sufficient information to answer that question (thus reinforcing prior training), or whether I need to use the time to instruct them so they can answer the question themselves.

Outside Pressures

In this age of instant communications, many things vie for control of your family. One of the most powerful shapers of thought today is television. A poll conducted by the *Washington Post* in 1978 showed that the average American, 18 years or older, watches three hours of television on weekdays and three hours, 25 minutes on Saturdays and Sundays. Other polls have shown that children under 18 spend two to three times the amount of hours their parents spend in front of the TV. (A graduating high school senior will have spent 5,000 hours in the classroom and 20,000 hours in front of the TV.)

Only one percent of those polled said they had no working television set in their homes; more than half said they had at least two working sets. TV has rapidly inundated people's lives, for a similar study conducted in 1970 showed only 31 percent of the nation's households had two or more television sets.

Over two-thirds of the people surveyed indicated that they watched at least some television every day, while 95 percent admitted to watching some television at least two days a week. Only 2 percent claimed no TV watching.

If you doubt that TV shapes American thought, fill in the blanks:

Don't squeeze the _____ (Almost anybody knows Mr. Whipple, the store owner.)

Double your pleasure with _____.

It's the real thing, what the world needs today, _____ _____.

Mrs. Johnson advertises which coffee? _____ (Fooled you. It's Mrs. Olson.)

TV is designed to make you dissatisfied with your life. For example, which of us is as understanding as the Waltons or as witty as Johnny Carson? Even parked in your driveway, does that new car ever look as beautiful as it did on the tube? Did you ever dream that your home could have "housatosis"? or that Uncle Charlie would know that you had a cat? Did those toys that the kids *had* to have for Christmas bring as much joy as they did to those kids in the commercials?

If you allow it to, television will dictate to your family how to dress, what house to live in, and where to spend its money. Learn to control the TV by limiting the programs that will be watched; discuss the commercials and how they attempt to arouse dissatis-

faction; don't eat in front of the TV (I'm probably the worst of-
fender of this rule, but the Lord dealt with me on it and I only
slip once in a while—actually, it's been very easy this last year
because we got rid of our TV!); use TV programs to launch family learning projects (follow up Wild Kingdom with a trip to the
zoo, or do some research about fencing after watching the Olym-
pics); and use the TV sparingly, not as a substitute for creativity.

The second most-prevalent pressure on your family will come
from peer groups—"Oh Mom, everybody's wearing (or doing, or
going to) it." If you succumb to such pressure, you will find the
outside world dictating many of your financial decisions.

I believe in a PPS (Parents' Protective Society)—whenever
one of our children proposes the "everyone" argument, we get the
name of at least two other parents and call them to check it out.
More often than not, the other parents also oppose their children's plans, but simply don't want to have their children become social outcasts. We have saved much money with such simple phone calls!

The last "everyone is going" argument we heard concerned a
back-to-school party for our high schooler. There were several
things about the arrangements that made us uneasy. After dis-
cussing it with Greg, he decided that the party did not fit into our
family's parameters for acceptable activities that we had agreed
upon, so he didn't go.

I felt very bad about his not going, so I arranged a family trip
that evening. A shopping center in our village of Kailua has a
musical light and water show called "Dancing Waters," so we decided to see it and then go get a treat. It was raining, but we
walked to the show (the weather is quite warm in the Islands).

Due to the rain, we were the only ones in the open air theatre
viewing the show that evening, but we greeted each number with
loud "ahs" and enthusiastic applause. At the end of the show,
the moderator announced over the closed circuit TV, "I don't
know who you die-hards are, but you've certainly made my evening!"

We continued through the rain, soaking wet, splashing each
other and crying, "Don't splash; you'll get me wet!" We finished
the evening with the planned treat.

The pay-off came the next day when I overheard Greg boast to one of his classmates concerning the party he'd missed, "That's okay, I had a lot more fun with my family"; he continued with a complete recounting of his family's watery misdeeds.

A third, and very subtle, pressure on your money decisions can come from your friends and the parents of your child's friends. Their reactions toward you when they discover how much (or how small) of an allowance you give your child will often put pressure on you when you least need it.

We are very selective with whom we let our children associate, so this is not usually a problem with us. We insist on meeting every one of the kids' friends, and usually go to meet the parents. Since our children attend a Christian school, most of their friends are Christians, and this helps to minimize the problems.

You have to decide who is going to make the financial decisions in your house. Will it be the TV, your child's peers, your neighbors, or *you*? Since God has given you written guidelines, I believe that *you and your Bible* can do the job best.

3

Three Essentials of Success

The Family Budget

Notice that the title is *family* budget. I'm astounded that parents spend 18 to 20 years preparing a child for his career, and less than three hours training him how to manage the money and possessions that his career will generate.

Involvement in the family's finances will provide your child the training he needs. By having the child participate in the family budget process, you accomplish several things. First, you are training him in the mechanics of family living and priority-setting. Second, you teach your child ways to stretch the dollar. Third, you help develop family unity.

In my opinion, family unity is, by far, the most important lesson your child will learn. Money, and money issues, will either unite or divide your family, depending on your attitude and how you convey that attitude to your children.

Recently, while staying in a motel in Bakersfield, California, I turned on the television. Phil Donahue was interviewing a Ph.D. about his book on money and families. As audience members asked questions and made comments, I became even more convinced of the need for families to work together. Individuals whose parents had taught them about money spoke warmly of their family life; those whose parents neglected this aspect seemed bitter about their early years. Some of their stories reminded me of our family.

Every summer, our kids are responsible for coming up with their own money to attend church camp. My wife and I provide many of the earning opportunities, but living in an agricultural area provides them the opportunity to learn how to work for others.

As the week for camp neared two years ago, it was obvious that Margaret Mary wouldn't have enough to pay for camp by the time she was to leave. A family meeting resulted in the MacGregors (including Mom and Dad) rising at 5:00 a.m. to pick berries for Margaret Mary's camp money. We all felt a part of Margaret Mary's life. (Frankly, it would have been easier for me to just give her the money she needed, but we would have lost the pleasure of working together, as a family, toward a common goal.)

An outstanding memory of my own childhood is that of a family camping experience. It was made especially memorable because my brother and I helped Mom and Dad pick avocados one Saturday to earn the money to buy the stove and lantern we used. We didn't feel poor; rather, Rob and I were excited because we were able to work with Mom and Dad toward a family goal. I've never asked Dad, but I suspect that we could have afforded to buy the items—I'm glad we worked for them!

Those "together" efforts your family makes to meet a financial goal will be rewarded, not simply with financially competent children, but with appreciation from them when, as adults, they see their peers suffering from their lack of training.

Tithing*

Each child should learn, very early, to tithe his income. Do not *give* your child money to put into the offering plate or Sunday school offering. Consider David's example in 2 Samuel 24:24: "I will not offer burnt offerings to the Lord my God which cost me nothing" (NASB).

Make sure that a tenth of his earnings is kept out and given to

---

*For more on tithing, see *Your Money Matters*, pp. 42-57 (Bethany Fellowship, Minneapolis, 1977).

the Lord on a regular basis. This has been mandatory in our family until each child reaches 13; then it is up to him. If I have trained my children right, they will continue tithing. (I still review their budgets on a regular basis and make sure that there is a provision for the tithe—I no longer make sure they put it into the plate, for at some point, they must answer to God individually. We chose 13 because it was the biblical age of manhood.)

The 50/50 Dad

In the previous chapter I told about helping my two oldest boys save money for bicycles by matching their earnings with an equal amount. My purpose, though, is not simply to help them reach their goals in half the time; this system goes deeper than that. *I am in for 50 percent of everything my kids are involved with—good or bad.*

Greg just received his learner's permit the other day (yes, I will accept all prayers!). As the day approaches that he will attempt his "solo," I want to reassure him that I'm his 50/50 Dad. Just as I paid for half of the window that was broken, and half of the iron that was broken, and half of the gas tank that was filled with sugar, I will also be ready to pay half if he does something to the car.

I want my kids to know that I love them—unconditionally! I'm still disappointed when they do something careless, or thoughtless, and I express my disappointment to the kids—but I don't disown them. When I think of the things that I've done, and yet my heavenly Father still loves me, can I do any less? I disappoint God, but He doesn't kick me out of the family.

I will be in for half of their first cars. I will pay for half of their college educations (theirs can be earned through scholarships, savings, working or ???). But most important, I will be 100 percent their dad.

PART II

Challenges in Money Training

4

To Give or Not to Give—Allowances

The subject of allowances is guaranteed to generate spirited discussion whenever and wherever it is brought up. The word itself denotes something that is allowed, and is used to describe various methods of providing money for a child. Let me describe some of these methods.

One approach is the "handout" method. People who favor this procedure argue that the child is part of the family and should have needs met as they arise. There is no regular, planned amount—the basic problem with this approach. Since the child does not know how much he will get, he can make no plans toward saving or spending. The child cannot learn responsibility in managing money—how to balance spending with income. This method also encourages a child to ask for money continually.

One of my buddies in high school, named Bob, had learned to "work" his mother for large handouts. It was amazing to watch him wheedle, beg and browbeat his mother into $15 or $20 for an evening out. I must admit that I enjoyed double-dating with Bob because he could always be counted on to throw extra money into the pot—it didn't mean anything to him. Since all my money was earned and budgeted, I was much more careful in my expenditures.

If you've been using the "handout" method, I suggest you keep track of the money you give out; you'll probably find that it's more expensive than a fixed amount would be. If your income is irregular, which makes a regular allowance seem impractical, put some savings aside to pay the children during low-income periods. The important thing is for the child to learn systematic management of money. (In your own budget, you should allow for saving money during peak periods to provide for slower times. This "normalization" of income makes budgeting possible, and will save you money in the long run.)

A second approach is a *fixed amount* of money *with no responsibilities*. Since one of the aims of an allowance system should be to teach proper management skills, this system is more commendable than the first method. The child will have a predictable amount to work with, but he does not become familiar with the *reward/penalty system* that the world operates on. I can't imagine one of us keeping a job long if we didn't do the work that was expected of us. Giving a child money and expecting nothing in return is a deficient method for teaching responsibility.

To teach job responsibility, some parents resort to a *job-rate system*, in which each job is assigned a value—$5.00 for mowing the lawn, $1.50 for washing the car, $2.00 an hour for housework, etc. How much the child earns depends on him. While this system teaches individual responsibility, it does not guarantee a fixed income that must be managed.

The approach that my parents used, that we now use for our children, combines elements of the last two plans into what I call an *allowance/earnings system*. It provides for a fixed amount that will always be given, plus a variable amount that is tied to responsibilities.

The fixed amount is the money given to meet the children's needs, as worked out in our family conference. We just completed our labor/management negotiations for the new year, and found that inflation required some adjustments—we try to review our children's budgets at least twice a year. The variable portion is for the fun things in their budgets (see the budget forms in chapter 9).

My brother and I were each paid a nickel a day for making our beds, a nickel a day for washing the evening dishes, and 50 cents for a weekend chore, which potentially gave us $5.00 a

32

month. If, for some reason, we didn't pass room inspection, we were docked 5 cents for the day, but still had to clean the room when we returned from school. The deductions never came from the "needs" part of the budget—always from the "fun" portion.

Some parents feel that an allowance should not be withheld to influence behavior—that somehow this is bribery. Dr. James Dobson makes some excellent comments about the "bribery" concept.

> Adults are reluctant to utilize rewards because they view them as a source of bribery. Our most workable teaching device is ignored because of a philosophical misunderstanding. Our entire society is established on a system of reinforcement, yet we don't want to apply it where it is needed most: with young children. As adults, we go to work each day and receive a paycheck on Friday. Getting out of bed each morning is rewarded regularly. Medals are given to brave soldiers; plaques are awarded to successful businessmen; watches are presented to retiring employees. Rewards make responsible effort worthwhile. The main reason for the overwhelming success of capitalism is that hard work and personal discipline are rewarded materially. The great weakness of socialism is the absence of reinforcement; why should a man struggle to achieve if there is nothing special to be gained? The most distasteful aspect of my brief military experience was the absence of reinforcement; I could not get a higher rank until a certain period of time had passed, no matter how hard I worked. The size of my paycheck was determined by Congress, not by my competence or output. This system is a destroyer of motivation, yet some parents seem to feel it is the only appropriate one for children. They expect little Marvin to carry responsibility simply because it is noble for him to do so. They want him to work and learn and sweat for the sheer joy of personal discipline. He isn't going to buy it!*

Guidelines for Allowances

To be effective, an allowance system should:
1. Be a regular fixed amount—with some variable portions.
2. Have elements of responsibility tied to it.

---

*From the book, *Dare to Discipline* (p. 59) by James Dobson, Ph.D., copyright © 1970 by Tyndale House Publishers, Wheaton, Ill. All rights reserved. Used by permission.

3. Be worked out in advance between you and your children.

What Expenses Should Be Covered in the Allowance?

This question will be discussed in Part III. Basically, parents should talk over and arrive at a mutual understanding with each child, regarding which items are to be covered by the allowance, which items are to be provided by the parents, and which items are to be earned through outside income.

At What Age Should the Allowance Start?

As soon as a child learns to talk, he learns the "*I wanna's*"— "I wanna candy bar," "I wanna ice cream," "I wanna toy."

This is the age to begin to teach responsibility. Although the age varies at which a child can attempt an exercise in minor money management, it will generally be somewhere between three and five.

How Often Should Children Be Paid?

For the younger child, two or three times a week. As the child matures, change to a weekly or even monthly schedule. (Perhaps it will be best to correspond it with your pay frequency.) The important thing is to make it regular, so discipline can be learned. (You will note that the forms in Part IV are weekly, but can easily be used for bi-weekly or monthly recordings.)

How Much Money Should Be Given in the Allowance?

The amount will vary with the age and readiness of the child, his needs, family circumstances and income, and the willingness of his parents to teach good money-management habits. The money should be more than just enough to cover his needs (lunches, bus fares, haircuts, etc.). It should include some discretionary income that must be managed—enough to give your child freedom to plan, and make a few mistakes, before the mistakes are too costly.

The amount needs to be *fixed* and *regular*, so the child can learn to balance spending with income. (We'll look at budget forms later.)

Remember, your goal is to *teach responsibility* in saving and spending money that is rightfully his. In the very early years, five or ten cents twice a week will be sufficient. As the child learns, this amount will be increased until he is responsible for managing even his annual clothing budget.

We gave Greg and George the responsibility for their socks and underwear when they were in seventh and fifth grade, respectively. We had to stay on top of George to make sure he spent his allotment properly. (He's just discovering girls, so is taking much better care of his appearance. Until now, his verdict of, "This undershirt is okay," did not quite match his mother's and mine.) But I experienced a degree of pride when he chose ten pairs of identical socks with the idea that a hole in one would not mean the retirement of both! However, we've had to put up with one of the loudest blues you have ever seen! But that's part of the exercise—letting him learn color coordination the hard way.

When Should an Allowance Be Discontinued?

Since I advocate an allowance that is earned, rather than doled, and since I believe that our children should be taught responsibility in handling money, I think our children should receive a regular paycheck from us until they are earning a full-time income, and thus able to pay room and board.

Life does not offer free rides, so allowing a child who is earning a wage to live at home without paying anything toward his support does everyone a disservice (of course, an exception would be when the wage is going to pay for a college education or some special purchase that the whole family has agreed on as a priority).

I once counseled a mother whose 19-year-old son was still living at home. This mother had four younger children still at home, and the oldest boy was constantly complaining about the lack of his favorite foods at the dinner table, and the wrong kind of furniture in the living room for entertaining his friends.

Upon questioning her, I found that her son was not contribut-
ing anything to the family support, but spending all his money
on girls and a 280Z! You would be surprised how many times I
have heard similar stories of irresponsible wage-earning children
living at home.

I do realize that this principle can be misapplied. One of my
friends, when he was 13, decided he wanted to attend a Christian
school rather than the public school. Don's parents were from
families in the Midwest, and had little formal education; when
they were old enough to work, they were expected to quit school
and work on the family farm. Don's father explained that paro-
chial education would cost extra, so Don would be expected to
pay his share.

At this point in the story, I nodded and agreed that this might
have been a good move (I remember that my own college career
took a drastic turn for the better when I had to start earning part
of my expenses), especially in a farming community where there
is much opportunity for work; but my agreement turned to in-
credulity as the story continued.

From that point, Don's parents kept track of every cent that
was spent on him—his education, clothes, medical bills, mileage,
money for school activities, and even birthday and Christmas
gifts! After college and graduate school, Don began repaying his
parents, with interest, in monthly installments.

Since every one of Don's brothers and sisters had the same arrangement with their parents, Don had no thought that there
was any other way, but he was bitter about it. Since then, Don
has found Christ, and the Lord has healed his bitterness and enabled him to experience an improved relationship with his parents.

While I cannot defend Don's parents, I do understand. They
had received nothing free in life and had been earning their own
ways since before ten years old; naturally they assumed their
own children would pay their way, too.

I enjoy providing for the needs of my family. I would never
support such extremes as in Don's story, but I would be cheating
my children if I did not teach them how to earn and manage
money.

If collecting room and board from a working child bothers you, I suggest what one couple did. They put the money paid by their son into a savings account. Several years after he was married, this couple gave all this money back to their son and his wife to help them buy their first home—a home made possible because his parents had taught him financial responsibility.

Should I Expect Reports?

Absolutely! A child will never do what you *expect*—only what you *inspect*! You will need to work with your child regularly, helping him to keep accurate records and making sure that the goals he sets are reasonable and attainable. This will probably motivate you to keep accurate records of your finances; your child is never going to let you get away with requiring him to keep accurate spending records if you're not keeping them too!

5

Paper Routes, Lawns and Other
Part-Time Jobs for Mom

For those of us who have children with outside jobs, our involvement is a fact of life. Allowing one of the kids to work outside the home requires a family commitment to cope with illness and conflicting school activities. (My prayers for Greg while he had his paper route were not entirely unselfish, since I was his number one substitute.)

I remember well the time both my brother and I were ill, and Dad had to deliver over 400 *Shoppers* all alone. He received much love and appreciation as he dragged himself in at 8:30 that evening. (Our supervisor chose that week to evaluate our performance, and we scored perfectly in every category except timely delivery!)

I was taught early in my life to work for extra money. My brother and I sold Christmas cards and decorations in the fall. We washed windows in late winter and early summer. We mowed lawns during the summer. We had a "house-sitting" service during vacation seasons.

I learned that to earn money, all you have to do is *find a need and meet it*. Because of those early lessons, I will always find a way to meet the needs of my family—even if it means taking a job "below me."

It is imperative for parents to teach their children how to

work. It certainly takes more time and effort than just handing the money to them, but the benefits are so worthwhile!

There are two things we must acomplish in our children's lives if we are to be successful parents. One, we must teach them to *feel good about themselves*; and two, they must learn that *they are responsible for their own actions*. Learning to work is essential to both aspects.

Two types of counseling situations always bother me. The first is when I face an individual who is out of work and complaining that he cannot secure a job. More often than not, he has job opportunities, but, "It just isn't enough money"; or, "I'm more qualified than that"; or, "With my back (hand, leg, eyes, arm, etc.) I just can't handle it."

These are legitimate excuses, but when they are used over many months, while the family continues on welfare, then I think it is time to examine the person's basic attitudes. Too often, the person harbors a mistaken view of job "status."

In Genesis 3:19 we read, "In the sweat of thy face shalt thou eat bread" (KJV); Proverbs 14:23 states, "In all labour there is profit" (KJV); and, Proverbs 22:29 tells us, "Seest thou a man diligent in his business? He shall stand before kings; he shall not stand before mean men" (KJV).

I'm not sure that the concept of *status* in a job is legitimate. Proverbs tells me that doing *any* job *well* brings me before kings. Joseph didn't start out as the number two man in the kingdom. He was a slave, then became overseer of Potiphar's house, only to be falsely accused and thrown into prison. Rather than lament his misfortune, Joseph remained a dependable worker and was soon put in charge of all the other prisoners. It was from this prison that he was appointed as the prime minister of Egypt.

When I teach seminars, I am often accused of relegating mothers to second-class positions, and not admitting that they can handle professional positions. This is not true; it just depends on your point of view. I suggest making things in one's home—I can introduce you to a woman who started a three million dollar business in her home. I mention typing part time at home—I know a woman who started a three-city secretarial business in her house. Doing a job the best you can is all the status you'll need to stand before Kings—and especially the King of Kings.

The second counseling situation I dislike is having to advise a businessman when his Christian employee is a slothful worker. One Christian employer I know (a very successful man) has hired more than a dozen "brothers" but has fired all but one of them. This man is only a new Christian and cannot understand why his non-Christian workers are much *more dependable* than the Christians. I don't understand it either.

Paul, in 2 Timothy 2:15, emphasizes that a Christian should be "a workman that needeth not to be ashamed" (KJV). I intend to teach my children to be good workers.

I take delight in giving more than is expected of me—in any job. I'm trying to teach my children to acquire the same attitude, because I believe that is how Jesus would work if He were here. My various employers have not always rewarded me for my extra efforts, but I have the satisfaction of knowing that I did the best job possible—and that the Lord knows and will reward diligence.

Last summer my brother hired my boys to mow his lawn and do some light yardwork. When they had finished, I inspected and found the job unsatisfactory.

"But," they exclaimed almost in unison, "that's all Uncle Rob wanted us to do!"

I explained that although this was true, I felt Christ expected them to go the second mile. I had the boys spend an extra hour doing the edging nicely. When they were done, they had the satisfaction of looking at a sharp lawn job. They were proud to know they had done one of the best jobs that lawn had ever received. Their second reward came when Uncle Rob gave them each a five dollar bonus for the outstanding job.

As an employer, it has several times been my unhappy task to "let an employee go" (a gentle expression that eases one's conscience after firing someone). Almost without exception, the employee was relieved! We know when we are doing a job well, and it feels good. We just as surely know when we are doing a job poorly, and that is a terrible feeling.

One of my happiest moments was when an employee came to me and informed me he was doing an insufficient job! Dave had been doing the best he could, but constantly fell short of the mark. He explained that his father had always told him to do the best job he could—and be the first to admit it if he came up against a job he could not handle.

Together we evaluated his skills and concluded that accounting was not his field. Today, Dave is a very successful computer systems salesman. He told me laughingly that one of his greatest assets in dealing with customers was his experience in a CPA office.

Dave's father had taught him to feel good about himself, and to do the best he could in any situation. He had also taught him responsibility. It would have been easy for Dave to find some excuse for not doing the job right—I hadn't given him the right instructions, I was gone from the office too much, I was expecting too much, there were too many distractions in the office, etc. Dave chose, instead, to assume responsibility and come to me to see what the best plan of action would be.

There is always a sense of accomplishment when we accept a task and complete it successfully. Be it mowing a lawn, washing a car, or managing a large business, there is something wonderful about receiving a good report—a "Well done, thou good and faithful servant."

What Kinds of Jobs?

In the younger years, extra jobs for your child will most likely be around your house or the children's grandparents'. The earliest job outside the home that our boys undertook was selling Christmas decorations door-to-door.

Greg was six, George was four, and both wanted to buy gifts for Christmas. We went out to the forest and collected fir boughs and cones, then purchased some fancy candles on sale; at a local hobby store we bought Styrofoam and "snow." Our whole family worked and made centerpieces.

Armed with twelve decorations, we set out to sell. (One of the difficult concepts that I had to get through to the boys was that I was entitled to a return for the "front money" I had in each of the arrangements. We finally agreed to split the proceeds until I had been reimbursed, and it was pure profit from that point on.) The whole project was quite a pain! The boys began to lose patience if there were more than two minutes between sales, and George always wanted his cut as soon as the arrangement was sold. We all survived and the boys had their first taste of the free enterprise system.

How about a car-washing service? Armed with a bucket, car wash soap, and a chamois, two youngsters can be in business. (I like them to work in pairs because they tend to be mutually encouraging.) A charge of $1.00 for a wash and 75 cents for vacuuming is about half the current rate, and should generate some takers as the kids advertise door-to-door.

I started in the fifth grade selling greeting cards and Christmas cards door-to-door. By the time I was in the ninth grade, I had a crew of five working for me, and learned that one can also earn money from the efforts of others.

During the summer, lawn jobs and house-sitting services can be very plentiful. The jobs will involve Mom and Dad, because your supervision of the "house sitters" will be a key selling point. Our house-sitting service involved yard care and making sure the house didn't look deserted. We put the mail inside the house, as well as papers and flyers; we checked outside lights and night lights, and gave the vacationers a phone number to call in case they thought of something after they left.

The list of jobs is endless. The possibilities depend on the maturity and physical capabilities of your child, and how much time you are willing to devote to training and supervision. Again, it would be much easier to just give money to them, but the long-range benefits of aiding them in earning it themselves is incalculable.

What About Paper Routes?

Certainly no American institution has taught young men and women the basics of business the way paper routes have. The biggest problem with a daily route is the tremendous time commitment; not only the several hours each day in wrapping and delivering the papers must be considered, but also soliciting new accounts and collecting. Carefully evaluate the physical stamina of your child when considering the route, as well as the time taken away from other activities.

I have encouraged my boys to procure weekly routes (most communities have weekly "shoppers" that generate a profit of 25 cents per month for each delivery, or "throw-aways" that are one cent each). These weekly routes require discipline and teach management of time and money without tying the family to weekend restrictions that a daily route creates.

What About a Car?

As a child grows older, pressure will come for a job that requires transportation. The question of allowing a teenager in high school to own a car is a very difficult one.

I usually advise parents to not allow their high-schooler to buy his own car. The initial cost, insurance and operating expenses are so high that earning the necessary money leaves little time for much more than homework. High school is a time when a young person should have maximum freedom to develop socially and psychologically. Where is the time for athletics, clubs, and friendships if so much time is taken with a part-time job?

However, I feel that teaching your child to feel good about himself is one of your most important jobs as parents. Therefore, what happens if your son or daughter doesn't like sports or club activities? How about the boy that loves to tinker with mechanical things? What if your daughter wants to pursue an activity that cannot be coordinated with public transportation or is too inconvenient for Mom to act as chauffeur?

In cases like these, a car becomes more of a need. It would be here that my 50/50 policy would apply. I would allow the car to be purchased only when half of the price had been earned—I, of course, would match the amount. Thus, I would be half-owner of the car and have control over its use and care.

I believe, and teach my children, that their identity is in Jesus. I am ready, however, to aid their peer identity during the critical teen years. If ownership of a car will aid this identity, then I'm willing to help.

6

In Case Your Child Isn't Perfect . . .

When you begin to teach your child about money, it will become acutely obvious that he is human. Not only can he make mistakes, he can probably also exercise poor judgment and even—oh horrors, not MY child—steal. Prepare yourself for potential problems; you'll be more at ease, and your child will respect your good judgment.

Losing Money

Do you remember that sick feeling the last time you discovered money missing from your wallet? A couple of years ago, I woke up in my motel room and went to the dresser to check the time; I could not find my watch. After checking around a bit I concluded it was gone. Suddenly it dawned on me that my money and wallet were also missing! A quick call to the desk confirmed that there had been several thefts that evening.

After a little reflection, I began praising God about several things. First, I had not wakened during the robbery, so no physical injury had ensued. Second, I don't have credit cards, so I didn't have to cancel any cards or be concerned about monstrous credit bills. Third, as usual, I had very little cash and my travelers checks were safe since I carried them separately from my cash. Fourth, I had learned why the sign said "Put chain on door when retiring at night" (a practice that had been encouraged by my father, but ignored until then).

You will notice that I did not yell at myself for my carelessness. I did not condemn myself over what the loss could mean to my family, thus encouraging guilt. I did not vow never to entrust myself with money again. I was calm and sympathetic toward myself.

Contrast that with the time George, as an active four-year-old, had come to me in tears over the loss of his birthday dollar. I had advised him it would be best to leave it in the house and not take it outside. Since he insisted on carrying it, I had shown him how to put it into his pocket carefully, so as not to lose it; but there he was, in tears, without any clue as to what had happened to the dollar.

I was very unsympathetic, and I harshly berated him for ignoring my advice and for being so careless, despite my warnings. I finished my tirade with, "Serves you right for not listening to me."

Frankly, nine years later, my immediate feelings would be almost identical, but the Lord has taught me much in the intervening years. Nowhere in His Word does God approve my calloused reaction: Proverbs 15:1, "A soft answer turneth away wrath: but grievous words stir up anger" (KJV); Matthew 6:15, "But if ye forgive not men their trespasses, neither will your Father forgive your trespasses" (KJV). Do you see how wrong I was? Well, I'm learning, and just about the time I master this parenting job, my last one (Gordon Dougall joined us Jan. 18, 1980, so I've got several years) will be raised and out of the house!

If your child loses money, no matter how much you warned him, use the experience as a positive teaching opportunity. If you are angry, simply tell the child that you can't respond to him right now, then wait until you have calmed down. Empathize with him, let him know that you understand how it feels to lose money (unless you are one of those fortunates who has never lost any). Find out if he knows what happened to the money. Get him to tell you what he might have done to prevent the loss. If the money that was lost was for essentials, suggest ways that he can earn half the amount lost. (Here, again, I'm in for half of whatever my kids do.)

Hoarding Money

There is a vast difference between saving and hoarding. Saving money toward a goal is a process that Scripture encourages. Proverbs 6:6-8 tells us to consider the ways of the ant—verse eight specifically tells us that the ant stores food for use during the winter seasons. Teach your child to perceive future needs and save in order to meet them.

Hoarding, on the other hand, exhibits a lack of trust. Matthew 6:19 tells us, "Lay not up for yourselves treasures upon earth" (KJV). Whenever a person begins to set money aside, only for the purpose of accumulation, he faces several potential problems.

First, *it can be easy to look to the savings account as one's provider* rather than God (Deut. 8:13, 14). During the early years of my Christian walk, I was guilty of this practice. I would build up my savings account and then look to God to meet a need or validate a decision by providing funds. I found myself almost saying, "And just in case you don't come through, I've got the money stashed away." God wants us to depend on Him as our source.

Second, *hoarding can create greed*. This is the hallmark of the hoarder: his whole life is geared to making another dollar. Making and saving money is a measurable process and can become extremely addictive. I like the way Jesus describes it in Luke 12:20, 21 (Amp.):

> But God said to him, You fool! This very night they [that is, the messengers of God] demand your soul of you; and all the things that you have prepared, whose will they be?
> So it is with him who continues to lay up and hoard possessions for himself, and is not rich [in his relation] to God—this is how he fares.

Hoarding is a vicious taskmaster; it demands more and more, but is never satisfied.

Third, *it can endanger integrity*. Proverbs 28:20 in the Amplified warns, "A faithful man shall abound with blessings; but he who makes haste to be rich [at any cost] shall not be unpunished." If you make the accumulation of money your goal, you will tend to "cut corners" to make the next dollar. I have experienced the heartache of watching a Christian start a business and then destroy it because he lost sight of God's principles in his quest to acquire more money.

Fourth, *hoarding can result in barrenness of life*. In Mark 4:19, Jesus relates, "And the cares of this world, and the deceitfulness of riches, and the lusts of other things entering in, choke the word, and it becometh unfruitful" (KJV).

Whenever I think of the deceitfulness of riches, I remember the Winchester Mystery House in San Jose, California. Mrs. Winchester was a very wealthy woman who believed that as long as she kept building her house, she would live. The result is an incredible mansion with secret passages, windowless rooms, stairs that go into the ceiling, doors that open into walls, and a seemingly endless string of halls and rooms. At her death, the house passed to her heirs who sold the valuable furnishings; the house stood unused until it was turned into a tourist attraction—a monument to the fact that riches cannot buy life. What a shame Mrs. Winchester didn't know that eternal life is available without cost through the Lord Jesus.

Finally, *hoarding can result in a phoney sense of security*. I have counseled couples in which one partner had been taught by his/her parents to maintain a certain amount of money in the savings account as a security "cushion." There is nothing wrong with this as long as one is not using the savings as a substitute for trust in God.

Test yourself with this question: "If God told me to give the entire savings account to Him, would I do it?" If your answer is yes, then everything is okay. If your answer is no, then you may have the same problem as the rich young fool in Luke 12:16-21. Trusting in riches, rather than God, is spiritual suicide.

In money matters, as in everything in the Christian walk, you want to instill in your child a keen sense of *balance*. You want him to be prudent and save for those expenditures that you know are coming (it would be foolish for him to wait until two days before church camp to begin to earn money for his half of the fee), and yet, you don't want him to miss the joy of having God miraculously provide for his needs. (Having done everything he could to earn the money, your child might still be short five dollars to get to camp, and suddenly an unexpected job comes in to meet the need!)

Overspending Money

The purpose of establishing a budget and an allowance for your child is to teach him how to make responsible decisions. One way he will learn is through wrong decisions. For example, your daughter may have been saving money and spending within her budget, then impulsively go on a spending spree, leaving herself with no money for an upcoming church outing. Or else, your son may suddenly be broke, and you discover that his money for next week's lunches has been squandered on candy at school.

Should these children be given more money or should they be forced to suffer the consequences of not spending their money properly? Generally, *let them suffer*. I doubt that missing lunches for a week will stunt your son's growth, but it certainly will remind him of his responsibility not to spend his lunch money foolishly.

Your daughter may wail and moan that all her friends are going on the trip while she stays home. Your usual reaction would be to give her the money, but she will not learn that she is responsible for her actions. Are you going to be there to bail her out at 20, 30, 50? I made several wrong decisions in my life and had to pay the consequences; I am very glad that my parents taught me to handle such disappointments.

Make an exception in the daughter's predicament, however, if others would suffer because she wasn't there to fulfill some responsibility. In cases like this, it is best to allow her to take the trip and impose an alternative restriction to cover the "crime." Peer group acceptance is very important to children and I don't like to jeopardize that acceptance unless the restriction is absolutely essential. (If you had warned her not to spend the money because of the trip, and she spent it anyway, that would be rebellion; rebellion must be dealt with very strictly.)

Watch carefully so that your child does not spend too much on other people. What appears to be a very generous spirit may mask a very insecure young person who is trying to buy friends.

One girl that we know just went through a very trying time after stealing over $50 from her classmates on a Christian school outing. The girl comes from a fine Christian home and is generally well regarded by her classmates, but felt she was not well liked, so she constantly bought things for her friends.

Her father had the same problem that I, and many of my Christian brothers, have—spending too much time being successful in Christian work and not enough time reinforcing our children's self-images. The story has a very happy ending; the money was returned and the girl's classmates all assured her they were praying for her and her family daily—it's tremendous being in the family of God, where others are willing to love and help in times of trouble.

Stealing Money

Stealing seems to be an almost-normal process of growing up. I don't condone stealing—but you will find that most children do it at least once. If you discover that your child has taken money, you need to ask yourself several questions:

1. *Is my child receiving all the love and acceptance that he needs in his relationships with friends and family?* That was the problem with the girl mentioned above; she didn't feel accepted and was stealing to gain attention.

2. *Does my child have enough money to meet his needs?* Sometimes you can put subtle pressure on your child without even knowing it.

    Randy's older brother, who had a paper route, was constantly receiving praise from his parents on how well he spent his money. Randy, on the other hand, always seemed to be a day late and a dollar short.

    When Randy was caught stealing from his mother's purse, his parents discovered that they had unconsciously demanded more from him than could be expected with the allowance he was earning. Like so many second-born children, much had been expected of him because of the example of the older brother. Randy's parents re-evaluated his allowance and made changes to provide enough money to meet the needs they expected Randy to handle.

3. *Is he busy enough so that stealing does not seem exciting?* I can remember some of my own stealing experiences; I stole after I was old enough to know better, and almost always when I had enough money in my pocket to purchase what I stole.

I'm not a psychiatrist, so I can't analyze why I stole; I just remember the excitement and challenge of the moment. Fortunately I was never caught, but had I been, my answer to why I did it would have been, "I don't know. I just thought of it and I did it."

I am not saying that what I did was right; I simply want you to understand how a person feels when he does something wrong, even though he knows better. There is something about human nature that just wants to touch wet paint, walk on the grass, or pull the lever when the sign says, "In case of fire. . . . "

4. *Did he honestly know he was stealing?* One time one of our boys was caught eating from a bag of potato chips in the store. In trying to explain to the four-year-old that he was stealing, I realize that he couldn't understand why it was stealing. A little more discussion took us back to the previous store where free samples were being handed out and I had eaten some. He honestly didn't know he had done anything wrong (either that, or he was one of the most convincing four-year-old cons I've ever met).

If he has stolen, handle the problem promptly and calmly. Make sure your child acknowledges responsibility for his wrong actions. This is probably the most important thing you can do, for children must learn that they are responsible—not that Johnny told them to do it, or that Cindy does it too, or. . . .

My son George is the epitome of the *Living Bible's* rendering of Proverbs 16:2, "We can always 'prove' that we are right, but is the Lord convinced?" Getting George to acknowledge his responsibility in a matter can be difficult at times, but is always done before punishment is rendered.

It is always best to have him make restitution; having to go into a store and return a stolen item to the manager is an awe-

50

some experience. That experience normally cures the excitement of stealing. Even if the money has been spent or the item consumed, confession and restitution are in order.

Borrowing Money

Each of you has to face this issue on your own. Credit in the United States is a fact of life. In my seminars, I urge people to discard credit cards and operate on a cash basis. While I gain some converts, most people are entrenched in credit and borrowing as a way of life.

If you use credit, you are automatically teaching your children to use credit, so make sure you teach them properly. My parents did an excellent job of teaching us money management, but somehow, never got around to demonstrating the proper use of credit cards.

When I was first married, I almost ruined my family because I used credit to inflate our standard of living. With the cards I bought things that we really didn't need, and kept our balances up to their limits.

If you use credit cards, always pay the monthly bills *in full*. What I didn't know was that Dad and Mom *put their cards away* at the end of any month that they couldn't pay the balance, and didn't use them again until it was paid off.

Sometime your child will ask for an advance on his allowance. Generally, advances ought to be refused. If the allowance is adequate and well managed, there should be enough money to meet expenses that arise. But, there can be unusual circumstances when an advance is acceptable.

Several times in my career, it has been necessary for me to request an advance on my paycheck. I'm glad that my employers didn't have inflexible rules against it. At the same time, I know that frequent requests for advances would have been resented, and would have reflected on my ability to handle my finances, which in turn could have an influence on my career. How a young executive handles his personal finances will have a bearing on his advancement potential in the business community. Do you see how important it is to train your child properly?

PART III

Patterns for Money Management

Introduction to Part III

Each of these next three chapters contains a list and descriptions of methods for making money. I've divided them into age categories so that you can get an idea of what types of money-making projects will work for each category. Most of the jobs have been tested, by either my brother and me, or my children; some are ideas that I feel will work—but need to be tried.

Most of the ideas are ones that can make a child the envy of every adult, because each is actually its own little business. Many men and women desire to be their own bosses; the best time to start is when they are young so that lessons can be learned. When you're self-employed, you determine how many hours you will work, where you will work, whether you will have employees, and how much you will earn.

In chapters eight and nine, the job lists have been addressed to the child, since children in those age categories can read. Encourage your child to read the chapters so he can exercise initiative in starting his own business.

If your child is old enough to procure a "steady" job at a service station, drugstore or wherever, have him consider some of the jobs listed in chapter eight. I know many young men and women who have put themselves through college with their own business. Some of these young people have even made careers out of the business they started when young.

There are two very important principles I need to emphasize before I go further: persistence and advertising.

Decide What to Do and Persist

Before he reads these chapters, or before you give him any ideas, have your child list everything he knows how to do. He probably can mow lawns, clean bedrooms, make beds, wash dishes, vacuum, baby-sit, wash windows, decorate the Christmas tree, go on errands to the store, clean the bathroom, wash the car, help Dad with the yardwork, etc.

Are any of these jobs, that he already does, something he can do for others and earn money? The answer to this question, of course, is yes. Can you think of other tasks that people put off or don't like to do? Taking down the lights after Christmas, shoveling snow, raking leaves, cleaning gutters, taking down storm windows, cleaning windows, and painting fences are all jobs that can be money-makers.

Have other people indicated they might be willing to pay to have something done? Are there any hobbies he has that could be money-makers? Have you thought about special seasons and the money-making potential of each?

Now decide what jobs he is going to do. Don't worry about the others; you'll need to help your child stick to what he decides to do. Before he starts anything, agree together on how long he is going to stick with a job before he gives up and attempts something else. If you don't do this, you'll find that discouragement quickly sets in, and a switch is made before a project really has a chance.

Advertise

The key to success in any business is getting customers; the way to acquiring customers is advertising. Advertising can be done in many forms.

When my brother Rob and I had our lawn service, we used a dual method of flyers and neighborhood canvassing. We simply went to each door in our area and introduced ourselves with, "Hi, I'm Malcolm MacGregor and this is my brother, Rob. We live over on Herbert Lane and are looking for work this summer. We're available to do lawns and yardwork.

"Also, when you go on vacation, we will make sure that all

your mail is put indoors and that no newspapers sit outside so your house won't look like you are on vacation. In addition, we're available to do other clean-up chores around your house. Here, would you like this flyer with our name and phone number on it?"

With that, we offered them a 3" x 5" index card with our names, services offered, and our phone number hand-lettered on it (with today's fast-copy services, this could probably be done on 8-1/2"x11" sheets and cut down for a very reasonable price).

It is very important to leave one's name and number with people, so that they can refer to it at a later date. One printer in Portland, Oregon, used to advertise 500 business cards for $5.95. That could be an excellent investment.

Most local grocery stores provide bulletin boards for posting advertisements. Also try community centers, local retirement homes (which can be excellent places to find customers for the jobs we list), churches, and anywhere else that people congregate. How about going to a local shopping center and placing flyers under windshield wipers? (Check with your local authorities.) Better yet, stand near the parking area and pass out flyers; this provides a chance to meet the people personally.

For bulletin board ads, attach an envelope labeled, "Take one," and put 15 or 20 business cards in it for people to take with them.

The most effective form of advertising is *word of mouth*. That means that the first few jobs your child does will be crucial to his success, so make sure he does them well. The extra time and effort put into those first few jobs will pay off; his satisfied customers will provide good references as well as excellent publicity.

On the following page, I have several examples of advertisements for different jobs. Note that I have divided a sheet of paper into eight blocks. Information for the same business could be duplicated on all eight blocks, cut up and distributed. In many cities duplication is available for as little as four cents a copy, so 400 "cards" could be made for two dollars. Typewriting is best, but *neat* printing will be acceptable.

PLEASE DON'T SQUEEZE THE CHARMIN

Let *us* do those things for you! We all have chores we dislike to do. Well, your dislike is our profit, so let us help. We specialize in all household chores, but especially:
LAWNS
FLOOR-WAXING
ATTIC-CLEANING
WINDOW-WASHING
The MacGregors
Greg (15)   George (13)
Call 329-5804 day or night
References on request

MacGREGOR'S WINDOW SERVICE

Residential or commercial accounts

329-5804

Call us for a free estimate.
Greg or George MacGregor
329-5804

Why not call—it's free until we do the work!

HAVE MOWER—WILL TRAVEL!!

You grow it, we'll mow it.

Greg and George MacGregor
Kailua

Call 329-5804

CORAL CATCHERS

Two experienced coral hunters are available to supply you and your customers with local coral. Special orders welcome!!!

Greg and George MacGregor
329-5804

BABY-SITTING

Do you need someone you can trust to watch your children with the same care that you give?
Call me and I'll give you the names of some satisfied mothers.

Margaret Mary MacGregor
329-5804

REASONABLE RATES

BIRTHDAY-CAKE SERVICE

Ever wished you could give someone a beautifully decorated cake, but you were too busy and the ones in the store were too expensive? Cheer up!!

ONE-DAY SERVICE
REASONABLE COST
Call Margaret Mary at
329-5804
Free delivery in Kailua
Small delivery fee outside Kailua

PET-SITTERS UNLIMITED

If you're going on vacation, we'll give your pet all the love you would give him—and more!!! Call us for rates and a free tour of our facilities.

Margaret Mary
George   329-5804
Greg

MOVING?

We are experienced in setting up garage sales and packing household goods. Call us for a description of our services.

The MacGregors   329-5804

7

Cradle to Gray Hair
(Usually Kindergarten)

A child generally learns by one of three methods: (1) *observation*—observing what you do and mimicking; (2) *explanation*—having you clarify things for him; (3) *participation*—actually involving himself in the process of dressing himself, tying his shoes, unlocking the door, opening a savings account, buying some of his own things, etc.

A preschooler will learn a lot about money by observing you and others. His ability to reason, however, is quite limited; given a choice between ten pennies or five dimes, he will choose the pennies every time. Recognize his limitations in abstract thinking and you will minimize your frustrations when trying to teach your young business person about money and business.

But, as difficult as he may be to teach, the lessons are too important to be left up to chance. (I am currently working with Youth With A Mission in Hawaii, and am hoping to complete a K-12 curriculum for teaching money management to children in Christian schools.)

Your preschooler should be allowed to sit in on family meetings when you review the family budget. Pay attention to his comments, and respond positively; encourage him to ask questions and make sure that there is a category in the budget that relates to him—his allowance, a trip, weekly shopping, etc.

Even at such a young age, I think a child should receive some kind of allowance. In our family, we found that Dr. James Dobson's system works quite well. We used it with our oldest son until he was eight. Dobson provides these excellent guidelines:

1. The chart on the next page lists some responsibilities and behaviors which the parent may wish to instill. These fourteen items constitute a much greater degree of cooperation and effort than most five-year-old children display on a daily basis, but the proper use of rewards can make it seem more like fun than work. *Immediate* reinforcement is the key: each evening, colored dots (preferably red) or stars should be placed by the behaviors that were done satisfactorily. If dots are not available, the squares can be colored with a felt-tip pen; however, the child should be allowed to chalk up his own successes.

2. A penny should be granted for every behavior done properly in a given day; if more than three items are missed in one day, *no* pennies should be given.

3. Since a child can earn a maximum of fourteen cents a day, the parent has an excellent opportunity to teach him how to manage his money. It is suggested that he be allowed to spend only ten to twenty cents per week of these earnings. Special trips to the candy store or toy shop can be planned. The daily ice cream truck provides a handy source of reinforcement. Of the remaining eighty-eight cents (maximum) the child can be required to give ten cents in the church offering or to some other charitable recipient; he should then save about thirty-five cents per week. The final twenty or thirty cents can be accumulated for a long-range expenditure for something he wants or needs.

4. The list of behaviors to be rewarded does *not* remain static. Once the child has gotten into the habit of hanging up his clothes, or feeding the puppy, or brushing his teeth, the parent should then substitute new responsibilities. A new chart should be made each month, and Junior can make suggestions for his revised chart.*

When your youngster outgrows this system, you should switch to an allowance system such as I described in chapter four—an allowance with fixed *and* variable portions.

---

*Text and chart taken from the book, *Dare to Discipline* by James Dobson, Ph.D., copyright © 1970 by Tyndale House Publishers, Wheaton, Ill. All rights reserved. Used by permission.

"My Jobs"

November	14	15	16	17	18	19	20	21	22	23	24	25	26	27	28	29	30
1. I brushed my teeth without being told																	
2. I straightened my room before bedtime																	
3. I picked up my clothes without being told																	
4. I fed the fish without being told																	
5. I emptied the trash without being told																	
6. I minded Mommie today																	
7. I minded Daddy today																	
8. I said my prayers tonight																	
9. I was kind to little brother Billy today																	
10. I took my vitamin pill																	
11. I said "thank you" and "please" today																	
12. I went to bed last night without complaining																	
13. I gave clean water to the dog today																	
14. I washed my hands and came to the table when called																	
TOTAL:																	

There are a number of money-management lessons that the preschooler needs to learn. First, he should learn the principle of tithing, and, also, giving to those in need. When the child has actually earned the money himself, what he drops into the offering plate has much more meaning for him. Teach your child early why Christ said, "It is more blessed to give than to receive" (Acts 20:35, KJV).

Teach him to set money aside to save for specific goals. One of the best goals is gifts for others in the family. Each Christmastime, we would take our children shopping so they could buy presents for the family—always a traumatic experience! Times like those try the patience of the Job in every one of us! It was an annual battle to keep the kids within their budgets, get them to realize that their mother doesn't need dolls any more, and prevent them from disclosing what they bought for each other (Margaret Mary would always give clues and then cry if the boys guessed correctly).

The payoff came last Christmas when they did all their shopping alone, on an outing with a club. Each of them purchased practical, thoughtful gifts for each other and us—all within their budget!

Take your young children shopping as a learning experience. Agree in advance exactly how much he can spend (and make sure you are well rested). Here are some other hints:

1. Allow him some say in how much to spend. Discuss, in advance, some of the choices he will have to make.
2. Choose a time when the store is not too crowded. It can be especially fun if a salesperson waits on him as he makes his choice.
3. Encourage him to ask questions and have the salesperson explain the differences in quality. (On one such trip I learned that major-brand appliance companies make the Penney's brands—as it was explained to my five-year-old.)
4. Try to keep the trip short.
5. Explain why he cannot buy everything he wants. Tell him how *you* make choices between items, and why.
6. Let him make the final buying decision, no matter how poor of a choice you feel he has made. (It is his money and

he must learn to be responsible for it.) Dr. Werner Von Braun, during the early years of our country's space program, observed that we learned more from our mistakes than we did from our successes. The same can be true with shopping experiences.

JOBS

Jobs for the preschooler are not numerous, but if Mom and Dad are willing to be involved, they are available.

Floral Supplies

Go into any florist shop and you will see an array of decorative arrangements that contain dry plants, pinecones, acorns, nuts, etc. Your little entrepreneur can find many such items in the neighborhood. On vacation, keep your eyes peeled for interesting dried pods, seeds and weeds as you travel. A couple of paper bags can be used to gather many of these items. Take them to your local florist and see if he is interested in buying any of them (you will have to accompany your young salesman on this trip).

Ask if there are any particular items that the florist is interested in. We discovered that the large sugar pine cones were in great demand, so when we were on vacation in northern California, we gathered several boxes full that netted us some nice Christmas money.

My mother takes these "dingle berries" (an affectionate name given to the many pods and weeds that we have collected for Mom all over the world) and makes attractive centerpieces, wreaths, hanging basket decorations, etc. One Christmas, our children sold crosses and wreaths that had been made from these dried items.

If you find some unusual pods, cones, or seeds, send a sample to my mom and she will send you a quote on how much she will pay for them in quantity or where you can sell them:

Bern MacGregor
Box 82
Gresham, Oregon 97030

Paper for Florists

We knew one wholesale florist that used to pay us quite well for newspapers. We would take out all colored pages, half-sheets, and comic sections. We then opened up the sheets and stacked them in six-pound bundles which we rolled very carefully and tied. These rolls were opened up by the florist to wrap flowers for customers.

Paper and Bottle Recycling

Armed with a wagon, children can go door-to-door and collect paper, cans, and bottles. With today's attention on ecology there are many recycling centers where these can be sold. You will, however, need a place to store them until it is financially worthwhile to go to a center.

In the meantime, you will find that many people will give away bottles with deposits on them, so your child will be picking up some quick cash along the way.

Go to parks and beaches after a big holiday and you will find plenty of discarded aluminum cans. Not only will your child be making money, but he will be helping to keep your community clean, too.

Paper should be tied in bundles and taken to a center when you have enough. The next suggestion is a very profitable method for using newspapers.

Paper Logs

The government has just authorized over 20 billion dollars for alternative energy sources. With all this attention on alternative energy, and the high cost of heating fuel, many people now use fireplaces and wood stoves to heat their homes.

You can purchase a newspaper "log" maker (just some iron tongues to wind the paper, and some wire to tie it with) and be in business. Once you learn how to make them, you and your child can prepare 30 to 40 logs in an hour, and sell them for 20 cents to 50 cents each, depending on the price of firewood in your area.

Maybe you could submit a grant proposal and get a government subsidy (thus teaching your children that, to the government, money doesn't seem to matter)!

Seashells

We have spent many happy hours at the Oregon coast gathering seashells. These shells can be sold to individuals with aquariums or, if nicely arranged, can be sold in wall hangings.

Perhaps you can work with your children as they make plaques that include shells and driftwood. Take a long piece of driftwood and put your name on it in shells (use weatherproof glue) as a sample; then go out and take orders for name signs for homes or beach cabins.

If you can get cigar boxes, line the insides with material or contact paper, glue shells on the outsides in attractive designs and you will have created $4.95 (small box) to $8.95 (large box with fancy lining, such as fur—scraps from upholstery shops) "whatnot" boxes.

Coral or Lava Sales

These items are limited, generally, to tropical areas such as Hawaii, but can be good money-makers. Last Christmas my three dove into the surf and came up with over $30 in coral sales—in only three days of selling. After collecting the coral, we simply soaked it in a bucket of bleach and out came beautiful "tourist coral."

Several very attractive items can be made with the lava rock that is plentiful on the islands of Hawaii. One can wholesale it to the many gift shops, or obtain a permit to sell to tourists along the waterfront.

In almost every area of the world I have visited, there has been some plentiful natural resource that visitors wanted to take home as souvenirs. These items are often collectible by even the smallest children, and with a little help from Mom and Dad, can be put into a marketable form, thus starting your children out right.

Mistletoe Sales

This, of course, is a seasonal item, but one that netted my brother and me handsomely over the years. Armed with a pruning saw and permission from local landowners, we would harvest our crop the first part of December. Back home, an investment in plastic bags was all we needed to prepare small bags of mistletoe that we retailed for 50 cents a bag.

Ours always sold very well because we made sure every bag had plenty of sprigs and at least one with "berries." If you don't want to sell door-to-door (which we always found best), you might be able to get permission from a local shopping center to set up a stand at one of the store fronts (a sign advertising your wares will help save your voice, but don't hesitate to do a little hawking).

Stamp Licking

Green Stamps and Blue Chip Stamps seem to find their way, unlicked, into a convenient kitchen drawer. Somewhere along the line, these stamps must be glued into books before they can be redeemed, and if most women are like my mom and wife, this is their least-favorite part of trading-stamp collecting.

Your child could make himself available to put those stamps into the books for 25 cents a book, or even for a percentage of the stamps licked. Advertising this service may be a little tough; perhaps it could be accomplished with a circular that is passed out while the kids are collecting bottles and papers.

Lemonade Sales

The Great American Enterprise-Starter is still the lemonade or Kool Aid stand. Last summer our kids made good pocket money selling lemonade next to the 15th tee at Salishan in Central Oregon. We were staying with some friends at their condominium, and the kids came up with the idea (also see golf ball sales) to help fill their time.

You don't have to have the stand in your driveway or at the

corner (that's where mine always went best); perhaps you could get permission to sell it at the local park during ball games. When her older brothers were playing soccer in very cool weather, Margaret Mary took a couple of thermoses of hot coffee and earned both money and friends!

Golf Ball Sales

When the boys were quite young, they loved to go visit Grandpa. Having gained permission from the local pro, they would walk the perimeter of the nearby golf course each evening in search of stray golf balls. Grandpa paid them 10 cents for every ball and 25 cents for the "keepers." The boys always wanted me to walk with them along the fence (in the out-of-bounds area) when we would go to the store. That trip plus a check of the creek behind the store almost always netted them four or five balls that they could sell along the course for 50 cents to $1.00.

There was also a driving range associated with the golf course. Most of the driving balls were gathered by machines, but a good number always seemed to be hit over the fence and among the trees. The pro paid the boys one cent each for the balls that were collected in those out-of-the-way areas.

You will probably devise some other jobs as you initiate your little ones into the world of business. Please write to me and explain what they are and how they worked so I can include them in future editions.

8

First Grade to Sophistication (Usually 7th Grade)

This is my favorite chapter, because I think 6 to 12-year-olds are the most fun to deal with in money management. A younger child is very eager to learn, but has a very short attention span.

From age 6 to about 9, the youngster will not always make the wisest choices, but the explanations he will give you as to why he made a choice can send you into hysterics. One year I received a model boat for Christmas with the suggestion that if I didn't have time to put it together, I could get help.

During these years, your child is going to need much encouragement and reinforcement. When he decides to take on a job, it should only be after agreeing with you ahead of time what is to be done and for how long. You will find yourself spending a lot of time reminding him to do the job that he would "never get tired of doing"—on the second day. Try to avoid criticizing him and comparing him with siblings or other children.

One thing I noted about our three oldest children during these years was their inability to properly assess the time required to accomplish a task. I constantly had to sit down with them, review prior tasks, and have them estimate times based on similar, though not identical, jobs. As they turned 10 and 11, their estimating skills had improved greatly. (Now all we have to do is get Dad straightened out—I am constantly underestimating a job while overestimating my ability to handle it!)

A younger child is usually very unrealistic about how much he is going to be able to buy. I found that shopping with my kids was simplified by taking a pad of paper with us, and I would write down the things they wanted to get before we spent any money. After recording the prices, we would total them, compare the total with our resources, and start all over again! It didn't take long before the kids found that it was easier to budget a maximum amount per item. I believe that it is because of such shopping trips that our children are such good shoppers today.

I'm convinced this is the age from which the advertiser derived the slogan, "Mother, please, I'd rather do it myself." There were so many times that I wanted to just grab something from the kids and decide for them, so I could get home (unfortunately, there were times that I gave in to the temptation, which always resulted in my having to ask their forgiveness; I'm sure it's been tough on the kids, raising me), but resisting that urge usually resulted in excellent learning experiences for the children.

Probably the toughest experience of the latter part of these years is the tremendous herd urge—doing things and wanting things because "everybody is doing it!" Bill Gothard has some excellent material on teaching your child to stand alone. If you have not attended one of his Institute in Basic Youth Conflicts seminars, you need to; it will change your life. If you cannot go to a seminar, at least find someone who has gone and ask him to share what he can about helping your child. (Gothard places some very important restrictions on what can be shared, so please be understanding.)

Spending Plans

Let's list some general things that a child in these age groups might be responsible for.

Ages 6-9

1. *Tithes and contributions*—For the younger child, I feel this should be a mandatory item that you remind him of weekly.

2. *Christmas and birthday gifts*—The best way to prepare for these expenses is to have him save a token amount and plan money-making projects close to those dates. The time span between saving in February and spending in December is too long to be meaningful for a 6-year-old.

3. *Clothes*—You might start off with him being responsible to save toward one item of clothing, such as socks. This will give him experience in planning his own wardrobe and provide at least one shopping experience each year for clothes.

4. *Bus fare*—Normally, monthly passes can be obtained for these trips, so put the money in his budget and allow him to buy the monthly pass. If the money must be given daily, have him go with you to a store to get the required change; put it into a jar with his name on it so he can see the balance dwindle as the fares are paid.

5. *Lunches*—Weekly meal tickets are normally available at the school. Let him take the money each week to buy his own ticket. Make him responsible, and incur a "fast" week if he is careless with the money.

6. *Grooming*—Include at least one personal care item in his budget. If your child is as liberal with toothpaste as mine are, have him buy his own toothpaste and he'll begin to learn that "a little dab'll do ya."

7. *School supplies*—Put at least one school item in his budget and let him shop for it. If it is crayons, he will begin to understand that 59 cents does not buy the 130-color set! Buying his own pencils may motivate him to be more careful with his supply.

8. *Fun*—Make sure that there is some income with which your child may do what he wants. Hobby items, amusements, toys, comic books, etc., are things that he needs to make choices on.

Ages 9-12

Here the list is the same as above, but we also add some items. Instead of one clothing item, he will buy several; instead of one personal care item, he will be responsible for most of his own grooming supplies, etc.

1. *Club dues*—During this period, your child may join the Boy Scouts or Girl Scouts, or some other organization, so there will be weekly dues and outing expenses.

2. *Camps*—Annual church and scout camps are great experiences for kids, but can be very expensive. I found that by paying for half, and requiring the children to earn the balance, caused them to appreciate their camping experiences much more. If you have a tight budget, perhaps you will have to help your youngster earn all the money; just make sure you assist.

3. *Books*—One of the greatest favors you can do for your child is to introduce him to books. Find the subjects that your child enjoys and encourage him to join book clubs and read those titles. Only one of my children has been a "natural" reader; the other two were introduced to books and eventually discovered that reading could be fun. Dr. Seuss books can be a great starters for the early ages (especially since they are so much fun for Mom and Dad to read).

Example

This plan was worked out for the child by sitting down and talking it over with him. (The "Spending and Saving Plan" and other forms used in this section are discussed again in chapter ten.)

The following items are recorded in his *Weekly Spending and Saving Plan*:

Sunday school—This is the tithe and is simply one-tenth of his total income.

Building fund—The local church is involved in a building program and the sixth grade Sunday school class has decided to trust God to provide extra jobs to enable them to give $52 per member.

Christmas—This is a total of $65 for the year, of which $52 will be deposited in the Christmas Savings Club at the sav-

WEEKLY SPENDING AND SAVING PLAN

<u>1/19/80</u>
Date

	+Allowance	Extra Earnings	*Total
Tithes & Contributions:			
Church			
Sunday School	.85	.75	1.60
<u>Building</u>		1.00	1.00
Savings:			
Christmas	.25	1.00	1.25 S
Clothes	1.65	1.00	2.65 S
Church Camp	.50	.50	1.00 S
Personal Expenses:			
Bus			
Lunches	3.25		3.25
Haircuts		1.50 S	1.50
Grooming	.30 S		.30
School Supplies	.30	1.00 S	1.30
Fun:			
Activities	.50	.75	1.25
Books & mags.	.20 S		.20
Dues (Scouts, etc.)	.50		.50
School Annual	.20 S		.20
Totals	8.50	7.50	16.00

*To Weekly Spending Record
+This is the fixed amount earned around the house

ings and loan. The remaining $13 will be used for seven birthday presents during the year, each of which will not exceed $2 unless extra money is earned. The amount for Christmas is higher this year because Aunt Belle is planning to take the kids on a two-day Christmas ski trip with her church group—$18. The parents questioned the $34 for family Christmas gifts, but that is what their son wants to spend. *Lunches*—The school lunch costs 65 cents a day. The $3.25 will be paid each week from September through June. It was agreed that the money from days when school is out will be used for extra treats at school under his control, rather than trying to adjust the weekly amount for holidays (except for the Christmas break, when the money is turned in to Mom to supplement her food budget).

Haircuts—Mom has always done an outstanding job on the hair, but Mr. America's curly locks have become very important to him (at 11, yet!), so he wants to have it done professionally. The cost to make this trip every eight weeks is a little awesome, but at least he knows that Mom is available if his money runs short!

Grooming—Junior is responsible for his own deodorant, hair oil, toothpaste, and dental products (this is pretty easy, since the dentist gives him a new toothbrush, paste and floss with each semi-annual checkup Dad pays for), while Mom and Dad continue to pay for the special soap required for his skin allergy.

Clothes—At this point, he is responsible for four pairs of school pants in the fall and two more in January, six school shirts, ten pairs of socks, and eight sets of underwear, while Mom and Dad purchase shoes, his winter coat, and miscellaneous "Christmas supplements." The allowances for the above items require him to keep his eyes peeled for specials:

```
6 pants @ $5  . . . . . . . . . . . . . $30.00
6 shirts @ $4  . . . . . . . . . . . . . 24.00
10 pairs socks @ 75¢  . . . . . . . . 7.50
8 sets of underwear @ $3  . . . . 24.00

                                $85.50   ($1.65 per week)
```

In addition, there is a special ski outfit that he wants to buy, so he is saving $1 per week to have enough for the outfit by the Christmas trip.

Camp—Church camp will be $45 this year, and Boy Scout Camp will be $82. After discussion at the family meeting, it was decided that the boys would have to earn all their money for Scout Camp this year because of the family vacation planned for Disneyland. Actually, this would not be too difficult because the troop holds an annual Christmas tree sale; all the boys, and their fathers, are required to help sell to earn toward the trip.

In addition, the troop will have several work weekends during which the boys can earn more money. Junior's older brother has earned all his money this way for two years. If there still is not enough money, berry-picking season ends only two weeks before the camp.

School supplies—Junior has bought a number of his school supplies for several years, so he is now responsible for preparing a list of all items he feels he's going to need for the year and price them. The total came to a little over $15 for the year, and will be provided by Mom and Dad. In addition, he has decided he wants to purchase one of the new LCD pocket calculators with a clock and stop watch; this he will earn himself.

Activities—The activities budget is one of the hardest to pin down. (The family moved last summer, so is unfamiliar with its new school's program.) Judging by last year's schedule, it would appear that 50 cents a week will cover more than half the activities that Junior will want to attend.

Books and magazines—Junior subscribes to *Boys' Life* and buys books at school from the Family Book Club (Christian titles distributed by Successful Living Books). Mom and Dad encourage reading as an alternative to TV.

Dues—This pays the weekly Boy Scout dues.

School annual—This is only an estimate of the cost. If the final cost is greater than the $7.50 anticipated, Junior will have to revise his budget and pay the difference from his own earnings.

Junior's allowance will be $442 this year, or $8.50 per week, to be paid each Saturday evening. During the week, he is responsible to keep his room neat, make his bed each morning, wash the dishes each evening, and clean the bathroom on Wednesdays and Saturdays. These chores are tied to the $1.40 allocated for the "Fun" items. If the chores are not done properly and promptly, Mom will note the problem and inform Junior; up to 20 cents a day can be deducted from his allowance and must be made up in extra earnings. This week there have been no violations, so the entire $8.50 is paid.

Junior has a weekly paper route that earns him about $20 a month. During the summer, there are many jobs around the house to help earn extra money (lawn mowing, car washing, etc.); but, during the winter months, few of these opportunities exist, so Junior must look to the outside to make up the difference.

There are a number of ways to handle the monthly check that comes from the newspaper company. Since Junior's allowance is on a weekly system, Mom keeps the newspaper wages in her possession and gives them to Junior in installments each Saturday; since there are four Saturdays this month, he will receive $4.92 each time.

Junior will have to find other sources to earn $2.58 if he is going to meet his budget for this week. (He has noticed that his next-door neighbor just had a cord of wood delivered, so he hopes to earn $5.00 for stacking it for him.)

Having Mom keep a list of his money, and balances owed him, will aid Junior in learning to handle fluctuations in his income by levelling them out. As he gets older, he will handle this responsibility himself. In the meantime, all extra money earned is kept by Mom to allow Junior to work with a fixed budget until he learns the disciplines of the budget.

In planning the next week's expenditures, Junior has marked some items with an "S," meaning that these amounts will be put into a savings account since no expenses are planned in this category. Thus, $8.10 is deposited at the savings and loan (or bank or credit union, etc.) on Monday, and noted on the Daily Spending Record and the Savings Record (on the following pages).

The *Daily Spending Record* will aid your child in developing a lifelong habit of keeping track of where his money is going. Plan on spending time with him each Saturday (or whenever you decide to regularly pay the allowance) to aid him in totalling his expenditures and checking them against his plan.

The *Savings Record* allows him to see how much is in his savings account and among which categories it is divided. Note that the Christmas amount is quite low, which is as one would expect right after Christmas. "Clothes" has a total of $16.65 in it ($14.00 plus $2.65), which will be enough to buy the pants that he and Mom will be looking for on sale during the coming weeks. The pants purchase will not appear on the spending record, but will be deducted from the savings amount, much the way one deducts a written check from his checkbook balance. There is no need to total the amounts every week, but it should be done once a month and a TOTAL put in the date column as it is done on the first line of the example.

At the end of each week, you will fill out the Weekly Spending Record (p. 76) to compare your plan against actual expenditures recorded in the Daily Record. Note that the amounts put into the savings account have an "S" in front of them in the "Spent" column to indicate they have been put into the Savings Record and that future expenditures will be shown from the Savings Record.

If you are like most people, you'll find this very confusing at first, but if you work with this system for a few weeks, you and your child will find it rewarding. It is a new discipline for both of you, but once mastered, will provide a lifetime tool for sound money management.

Allow your child to open his own savings account and transact his business alone as much as possible. All our children have their own accounts at a savings and loan that is on their way home from school. I helped them open their accounts and went with them the first time they deposited or withdrew; now they handle all their own transactions and only check with me monthly when we reconcile their accounts with their spending records. (I work with my children on a monthly basis and feel that each parent should aim toward this as a goal—paying and budgeting monthly.)

DAILY SPENDING RECORD

1/26/80
week ended

	Tithes and Contributions	Saving	Personal Expenses	Fun
Sunday	tithe and building 2.60			
Monday		8.10	lunch .65	
Tuesday			lunch .65	Boy Scouts .50
Wednesday			lunch .65	
Thursday			lunch .65 eraser .30	
Friday			lunch .65	
Saturday				Show 1.25
Total	2.60	8.10	3.55	1.75

Cafeteria notice: extra 5¢ needed for large milk - talk to Dad about more money

SAVINGS RECORD

		Christmas	Clothes	Church Camp	Personal	Fun	Savings Balance
TOTAL Date	Saved Spent	3.75	14.00	22.00	20.80	1.42	61.97
1/21 Date	Saved Spent	1.25	2.65	1.00	2.80	.40	70.07
_____ Date	Saved Spent						
_____ Date	Saved Spent						
_____ Date	Saved Spent						
_____ Date	Saved Spent						
_____ Date	Saved Spent						

Shopping

So many lessons need to be learned for your child to become a wise shopper. One important lesson to teach your child is price differences between stores. Armed with a pad of paper and a pencil, go to a local convenience market and write down the prices of several different items; then check the items in a chain store—quite a difference! Finally go to a discount or mark-it-yourself store and compare the same products. One such trip revealed a 17-cent difference (34 cents vs. 51 cents) between identical cans of one brand of string beans.

If one of the managers in the local stores has time, perhaps he might explain some of the differences between the name brands and some of the store brands. (Many of the Sears, Wards, and Penney's brands are made by name-brand manufacturers, with little or no difference in quality.)

Let your child plan a meal and then help you shop for and prepare it. This is just as important for boys as well as girls, since many of the boys are going to be away from home and unmarried for a period of time. (I still enjoy shopping with my wife—when she will put up with my constant stops to compare and research.)

JOBS

Jobs for the pre-teen and teenager are much more numerous and require less of the parents' time. Some of the jobs that children start during these early years can easily develop into lifetime careers.

Paper Routes

This is one of the most common jobs for kids; the route can either be daily or periodic (three days a week or even weekly). The job requires a significant commitment from Mom and Dad because of illnesses (see chapter four), but will normally provide almost all the extra money your child will need. If he must earn extra beyond his route income, he has a whole list of potential customers who are already aware of his dependability (assuming he's done a good job on the route).

WEEKLY SPENDING RECORD

Totals from Daily Spending Record	WEEK 1 1/5 Date		WEEK 2 1/12 Date		WEEK 3 1/19 Date		WEEK 4 1/26 Date	
	Plan	Spent*	Plan	Spent*	Plan	Spent*	Plan	Spent*
Tithes & Contributions:								
Church								
Sunday School					1.60	1.60		
Building fund					1.00	1.00		
Savings:								
Christmas					1.25	$1.25		
Clothes					2.65	$2.65		
Church Camp					1.00	$1.00		
————								
Personal Expenses:								
Bus								
Lunches					3.25	3.25		
Haircuts					1.50	$1.50		
Grooming					.30	$ .30		
School supplies					1.30	$1.00 .30		
————								
Fun:								
Activities					1.25	1.25		
Books & mags.					.20	$ .20		
Dues (Scouts, etc.)					.50	.50		
School annual					.20	$.20		
————								
————								
Total					16.00	16.00		

Phone Directory Delivery

Each year the telephone company distributes new directories. Contact your local phone company and find out how it delivers them. If it's like the companies in our area, the books are delivered by independent contractors at a fixed rate per book. A call to our phone company revealed that the service was already contracted out for the year, but we spoke to the contract holder and found that he was looking for help.

Here's where a family partnership is necessary, for the company most likely will not contract with an 8 and 11-year-old, but will contract with Mom. After getting your territory, you must negotiate with Mom, since she is entitled to some of the money for her time and car expenses (she will probably have to drive the area and "cruise" while the kids deliver the books).

Advertiser Delivery

Many businesses insert multiple-page advertisements into the Sunday newspaper, especially during special sales. Everyone, however, doesn't purchase the daily or Sunday paper, so they miss such advertisements. This could mean profits for you. Go to one of these stores and ask if you could pass out their advertisers in your area for 2 cents each.

In our vicinity, a weekly advertiser is delivered by carriers; the same company distributes advertising supplements. In a small town, it might be possible to work directly with the local paper, since it will probably print any advertising "throwaways."

Try going to one of the local merchants that does advertising (especially if he has coupons in his ads) and talk to him about printing a limited advertiser for your area that you would pass out. One merchant in our area regularly sends such a limited advertisement to postal box holders. I've never approached the store manager, but I think he might be interested in having this limited advertisement delivered within a mile radius of his store. Perhaps you could talk one of your local merchants into a trial of this sort.

Sample Distribution

Several times a year, samples are left on my doorstep. Here's where a letter might gain you some money for delivering samples. Write to Proctor & Gamble (one soap manufacturer that distributes such samples) or some other similar manufacturer and tell them who you are:

Dear Sirs:

My name is George D. MacGregor. I am 13, and am in the seventh grade at International Christian School in Kailua-Kona, Hawai.

It has come to my attention that you distribute free samples frequently to introduce new products. While I recognize that you would normally only distribute samples in major market areas, it occurred to me that a capable and trustworthy representative on the Kona Coast could handle the delivery of 3,000 to 4,000 samples in a three-week period.

I have enclosed a map of the Kona Coast area that I feel I could adequately service for you, and an estimate of the population involved. You will note that I am proposing to service 1,000 residences and 2,000 to 3,000 tourists who will take the product back to their homes on the mainland, thus increasing the geographic dispersion of your products.

May I hear from you soon about your interest and the usual financial arrangements for sample distribution?

Yours truly,
George D. MacGregor

This type of letter will obviously need some help from Dad or Mom, but can be typed by the youngster himself; and I can assure you, the manufacturer *will* respond. I chose a national brand as an example, but you may know of a local manufacturer or regional distributor that would be a possibility.

You will also gain valuable experience doing some market survey work in the area and writing the letter.

Sample Assembly

My brother and I used to assemble samples for a San Jose, California, tile manufacturer. The company cut the tiles into small squares, then stamped a style number on the back of each;

they punched a hole in each one, and we chained them together. I don't recall how much we were paid for each sample, but the work was something we could easily do while watching TV, so it was "found" money. Perhaps you don't have a tile manufacturer in your area, but you might find something else (carpeting, paint, fabric, etc.).

Securing such a job will mean going to the plant and approaching the sales manager. Explain to him what you want. (When I say "you," I mean the child. I am assuming that Mom or Dad will go with him, but the experience of asking about sample assembly should be the youngster's.) Then ask if there is anything that you could do in your own home on a sub-contract basis to aid them in preparing samples. This type of initiative is not seen very often in young people today and will probably be rewarded. If the sales manager does not have anything that you can do, ask him if he can recommend someone who does (a referral sale is usually easier than "cold turkey").

Parent's Helper

This job is not only a money-maker, it could easily win you the lasting love of many a parent. I remember that many times, when our three were small, we would try to accomplish a cleanup task on a weekend; we were continually interrupted by the kids to do everything from finding lost toys to breaking up attempted homicides. If a reliable youngster from the neighborhood had offered to play with my kids and keep them occupied, I would gladly have paid him 50 cents an hour.

You might also be able to land a steady job helping a mother just before the evening meal. You could feed the baby, give the children their baths, and straighten up the house before the husband arrives; for a mother, this is usually the most hectic time (and when she is most tired) of the day.

Silver Polisher

This could be a great source of extra money during the holiday season. There is more than just silverware to be polished, but this is a good place to start to build your reputation. (Most families have a few pieces of silver in their home, so Mom can give the kids experience and gain a free shine by allowing them to start with her pieces.) Once you have perfected your technique, find a neighborhood where people do a lot of entertaining, and distribute leaflets advertising your service. I suggest charging by the hour; and advertise an assortment of party services too.

Party Helper

Parties are difficult to prepare for, especially if one has small children, so you could offer a complete party service or a selection of helps.

Setup: Decorate, run errands, get ice, clean the house, watch the children, prepare hors d'oeuvres, keep the dog out of the snacks, etc.

Serving: Serve the hors d'oeuvres, keep the ice bucket full, keep the nut dishes full, help in the kitchen, and *just be available.*

Cleanup: We would probably entertain people more often if it was not for the cleanup. What a let down, after a delightful evening with friends, to stand at the sink and wash dishes. As a cleanup person, you would completely clean up the kitchen and dining area while the host and hostess entertain; return the next day to wash the snack dishes, clean the entertainment area, mop the kitchen, and vacuum the house.

Charges for each of these services could vary, but should probably be marketable at $2 to $4 an hour, depending on your age and experience. If you're 9 or 10, you will probably be able to get only setup and child care tasks at 75 cents an hour, but good performance on those assignments will put you in good standing as you get older. I expect a young teenager could earn $30 to $40 by helping with a large party.

A note to parents: "parties," in these days, can involve a wide gamut of beverages and activities. Protect your child by screening potential clients. Make sure that a party will be up to your standards of decency.

Errand Running

This is a good job for someone in an area where there are many apartments and condominiums. Job potential is especially good where there are a number of older residents. In order for this to be a good paying job, you will need to advertise—this is where those flyers we talked about earlier will be useful. You will not gain many customers initially, but do serve them with enthusiasm and courtesy, and you will soon have many "clients."

The jobs you get will be little "run-around" chores, such as purchasing groceries, going to the pharmacy, picking up and delivering dry cleaning or laundry, or returning books to the library.

People may have you do these jobs for them because of physical or time limitations. (The dry cleaner near our house opens a half hour after I leave for work and doesn't have a night drop, so I might be a potential customer.)

Start by distributing your flyers to as many apartments as you think you can cover; return the next day and ask any potential customers, "Hi, I'm Margaret Mary MacGregor. I passed out a flyer the other day. Did you receive it?"

This will evoke a response, and you can take it from there. If the person says he doesn't have a job for you that day, say, "Okay, I'll stop by tomorrow and see if you need anything then."

Unless they ask you not to come again, you have a potential customer. Establish a regular schedule so that your customers predict when you will be there, and can plan the errands they'll have for you.

Pricing this service could be difficult. Try letting the people set the rates for you at the beginning to determine what an acceptable fee will be.

Ironing

If you're a boy, your immediate response will be that this job is for girls only. Mom taught my brother and me how to iron when we were seven and eight, and from that point on, we did most of our own ironing and picked up cash by doing other pieces for Mom. Since most boys will spend a few years in bachelor-hood, it is an excellent idea for them to learn to cook, sew, iron and clean. These chores, which may be reserved for the girls in your house, were the mainstay of my allowance as a young person, and I have been much help to my wife over the years.

An ironing service can be performed in your home or at your customer's home. Pricing could be from $1.50 to $3.50 an hour, or by the piece. (I found that charging by the garment gained me more customers and earned me more money.) An ironing service could coordinate well with the next idea.

Laundry Service

One of the most boring activities in the world is sitting in a laundromat, waiting for a load of washing or drying to be completed. For the working individual, this is doubly so, because he often has to wait for machines to free up during the evening and weekend hours, which are usually the busiest times.

Your best potential customers will be in apartments and condominiums, especially those that do not have laundry facilities (singles and young working couples are great prospects, even when they have laundry facilities). Since your afternoons are free, you will be able to use the laundromat during off-hours when everyone else is at work. Your charge for this service would be $1.00 to $1.50 per load. Have the customer furnish the detergent, or you could provide the soap, bleach and fabric softener for an extra 20 cents per load. The customer should be expected to pay the washer and dryer fee.

Pick up the laundry (along with hangers for the permanent press clothes) and cleaning supplies, as well as any special instructions each evening. The next day, wash and dry the clothes, carefully hang the clothes that require it, and fold the remainder in the manner that the customer desires (keep a list of customers and any special folding requirements—this little extra can mean great recommendations). Return his laundry that evening.

Good performance will earn you permanent customers—ones that you can count on each week. Assuming you can do an average of five loads per week at $1.50, you will earn $7.50 per week.

Doing a good job will also give you a chance to do other things for the same customers. Be alert to their needs when you call on them to pick up and deliver. (Help with a party that they mention they are having, do spring cleanup, run errands—the possibilities are limited only by your imagination and willingness to work.)

Dog Walking

Since I've always lived in areas where homes have yards, I have no practical experiences in this service, but I'm sure there is a market for it. Again, apartments and condominium units should be the best source of customers, since the occupants often work long hours and don't have a lot of extra time to walk their dogs.

This should be worth $1.00 an hour. If you had two dogs to walk, you could walk both at the same time (providing they don't hate each other) while running errands, delivering papers, or just jogging, and pick up an extra $2.00 at the same time.

Pet Sitting

Judging by the way some people treat their pets, this could be a gold mine! Even if you cannot find someone who dotes on his animals (Any time I think of doting owners, I think about Tricky Woo, the pampered dog in one of James Harriot's books), people are always looking for someone reliable to look after their cat, hamster, fish or whatever, when going away for a weekend.

Depending on the animal and services provided, you would charge 50 cents to $1.25 per visit (You would generally take care of the animal at its own home, although small animals might be easier to keep at your place), and extra if it involved walking a dog.

Pet Grooming

For this job you will need a tub, pet shampoo, brush, hose, and permission from Mom (shaking dogs make the biggest messes you've ever seen). This service can develop into a lifetime career, or can at least supplement your income as you get older. Charges for washing and drying a dog will vary with the size of the pet and what is charged by groomers in the area. In our area, $5.00 would be well below the rate for a medium-sized dog.

If you really get serious about this job, you can study books on clipping and full grooming and add these to your washing service. Price your work a little below the prevailing market, and you'll have steady business.

Pet Accessories

Graham Kerr (you remember the Galloping Gourmet) often cites some startling statistics that show Americans spend more on their pets every year than they do in supporting Christian missions. I'm making no comment on this—just pointing out that there is a tremendous market for pet products. Here are some that might earn you extra money:

Name plaques—possibly even with the meaning of the pet's name. This could be done in script or routed in wood.

I.D. tags—This would involve an investment in a machine that imprints on an aluminum tag. Such equipment could be taken from door-to-door.

Christmas stockings—a special stocking for Fido to hang out at Christmas (we've always hung stockings for our pets over the years).

Special collars—If you have artistic ability, you could do leather work on regular collars, using the pet's name or an attractive design.

Cat scratching posts—These can be made with scrap lumber and carpet scraps. Your cost can be almost nothing, and these attractive furniture savers are marketed for as much as $10. Just go to a pet shop and study their construction, and the price range—and off you go!

Shoe Shining

A luxury that I frequently indulge in is a shoe shine while waiting for an airplane! I've often wondered why some enterprising youngster in my neighborhood hasn't gotten this idea as a money earner. Armed with a portable kit, you could offer to do the job on the spot (or in cold weather, in the customer's house), or take the shoes back to your home to shine. Depending on the rates in your area, you should be able to get at least 50 cents a pair.

This would be great to offer with a laundry or errand-running service. If you do the job in someone's home, make sure you carry a dropcloth to protect the carpet. Attention to such detail shows your responsibility.

Berry Picking

Children in agricultural areas have the advantage of summer jobs (barring federal "child labor" legislation) where they can learn to work hard under close adult supervision. My brother, another young man, and I contracted with a local farmer to pick his five acres of prunes one summer.

Like berries, prune picking is done from the knees, and convinced me that being an accountant was more desirable, but I did learn to stick with a job, once I had contracted to do it, and I gained the satisfaction of earning a good sum during my summer vacation.

Coffee Picking

This, of course, is a highly localized job opportunity (the only coffee plantations in the United States are in Kona, Hawaii), but shows that many localities have some potential for agricultural jobs. Our family spends several Saturdays a year picking coffee to pay for a special vacation. Remember that earlier I mentioned Mom and Dad picking avocados with us in Southern California; our kids have picked berries and coffee, and my brother and I have picked all sorts of fruits. The possibilities seem endless.

Coffee bean picking, by the way, is fascinating. We were able to find several fields that have gone wild and sold the beans to a co-op at market value, netting the family over $100 for a morning's work.

Fruit Picking

Up and down the West Coast, in the Southeast, and in portions of the Midwest, I have seen apple, pear, peach, orange, prune and other fruit orchards converted to housing tracts for sprawling suburbia. Many times, the developers have left as many fruit trees as possible, thus creating an earning potential for you—many of the landowners simply let the fruit rot on the trees. Most people with trees are filled with good intentions that *this* year they are going to pick the fruit, but much of it will ripen before they admit that they have no time to do it themselves.

If you live in such an area, stay alert for trees that are becoming overripe and approach the owners about picking their fruit. Offer them a fourth of the yield and sell the remainder. Check local stores for current market prices and sell the fruit at 50 percent of retail to home canners (you might even be able to sell at 90 percent of retail on certain fruits).

Probably the best way to advertise is on supermarket bulletin boards. Try to secure advance orders for the fruit, explaining to callers that you are locating the product and will supply it as soon as you can.

Canning Helper

I have often helped my mother and my wife during canning season, so I know that it is much easier with a little help. Along with fruit picking, you might hire yourself out to help with canning by peeling, coring, chopping, washing jars, or simply keeping the kids out of the way.

The price of this service will vary with your age and experience, but I would imagine that $2.00 to $3.50 an hour would be a good range.

Vegetable Gardening

If you have a large yard, growing and selling vegetables can be an excellent money-maker. Several crops, such as tomatoes, produce large yields in a small space. If your climate and soil are right, such a cash crop will bring many eager buyers, since the quality and size will normally be superior to that found in a store.

Those of you in rural areas should consider the example of my cousins, Phillip and Larry Glashoff of northern California. As young teenagers, to expand their small garden plot, they leased land from a local farmer and planted five acres of pumpkins which they successfully wholesaled to local merchants. (They also retailed by advertising the pumpkins in the local paper.)

This humble beginning has mushroomed in recent years into a flourishing business. Many West Coast pilots are familiar with the Nut Tree Restaurant in Vacaville, California. Across the freeway from this famous restaurant, you will find the Glashoff Brothers Fruit Stand where Phil and Larry market products grown on their own plots, as well as products purchased from local wholesalers.

Herb Gardens

Those of you with green thumbs, and no land, should consider the many herbs which can be raised in trays in your basement. One of our friends has several sprout boxes in his basement that produce rapidly. He wholesales to a local food chain. His enterprise began as a desire to have fresh sprouts for his own use and soon expanded into a full-fledged business. A trip to your local florist will inform you as to what herbs can be grown in small spaces and the potential market for them.

Lawn Mowing

Lawn mowing is a perennial money-maker—and certainly one that has paid off handsomely for the MacGregor boys over the years. In some of the southern climates, this job has year-round potential, and has the advantage of producing steady and dependable income, since once you get a satisfied customer, you will likely be able to keep him.

Price this service either by the hour or by the job. Professional lawn cutters in our area earn between $7.50 and $11.50 an hour.

Check the going rates in your area and charge accordingly. Once you have landed the job, you can figure an average of how long it takes and eventually establish a flat rate.

Typically, lawn mowing will entail cutting, raking and edging, but it can open up opportunities to do a myriad of other yard chores for a satisfied customer—and that satisfied customer will be your best advertising. A neighbor who sees you doing a consistent job, week after week, is going to call on you when he decides to have his lawn done.

I always liked it best when a customer provided his own mower and tools, because I didn't have to drag mine around with me. After you have been doing lawns for a while, you may want to invest in some professional equipment of your own. This equipment has a longer life than regular equipment, and normally allows one to do a quality job in a shorter period of time.

Weed Pulling

If there is one job I hate, it's pulling weeds, but it earned me one of the first paychecks I ever earned outside my home. A neighbor was out pulling weeds and about five of us descended on him looking for work. He assigned us to a flower bed. Over the next 30 minutes my cronies silently disappeared; I was soon the only one left!

I don't remember how much the man paid me, but it took almost a week of working after school to complete the job.

Pulling weeds is a drudgery, so don't take on this job unless you're willing to stick with it. However, since adults, the world over, seem to loathe this job, you should be able to earn the same two to four dollars an hour you could earn cutting grass.

Leaf Raking

While songs about autumn leaves sound pleasant, raking leaves can be a real chore. The raking season is very short, but can gain you valuable contacts for other services during the year (see snow shoveling, Christmas lights and wood stacking).

Charge the same as for weed pulling. Service should also include bagging the leaves for trash pickup.

Barkdust Spreading

In the Northwest, and other lumbering areas, barkdust, a by-product, is available in large quantities. Many landowners order an annual delivery of barkdust and chips to spread on their gardens. (It not only looks nice, it helps control weeds and makes weed pulling simpler.)

Normally local firewood dealers also handle bark delivery, so contact them first and ask them to give your card or flyer to anyone ordering in your area. When a customer responds to your ad, go to his home and give an estimate for the job. One nice thing about barkdust is that two or more families will often go together on an order, so you may have more than one potential customer for each delivery.

Lawn Edging

This service would normally be offered with your lawn service, but could be marketed separately. Often, an individual mows his lawn but doesn't seem to get around to the "cosmetic extras." Especially around sidewalks, edging left too long can really build up.

Check your local paper for moving sales and you will often be able to pick up an electric edger for under $20. Armed with this edger, scout your local community for lawns that need your service and knock on the owners' doors. Your sales pitch might go like this:

Hi, I'm Greg MacGregor. I know my dad tries to keep up the lawn, but every once in a while, the edging gets away from him and it's quite a chore a get it back in shape. As I was passing, I noticed that your edging reflects your busy schedule, so I thought I'd offer my services to help you catch up. I have a power edger and would be happy to edge and then clean up for five dollars.

Set your price according to your experience and how long you expect the job will take. If they refuse, make sure you leave your name and phone number in case they reconsider—they may also think of you if other chores come up.

Furnace-Filter Replacing

Studies indicate that a consumer will save close to $30 a year by changing the filters on his furnace every two months. In the years that we heated our home with oil, it seemed that I constantly forgot to change the filters in our furnace. I would have gladly paid someone $2 every two months during the heating season (about $8 a year), plus the cost of the filter, to come and change the filter for me.

If you had sixty customers, you would clear $480 a year with very little effort. Watch for sales where you can sometimes purchase furnace filters at one-third of their normal retail price, and keep an inventory on hand. You could charge double your price and still save your customers money. (If you cleared 25 cents per filter, you could pocket at least an extra $60 depending on the filters each furnace needs.)

You may also be able to offer this service for central air conditioners during summer months, or year round in warmer climates.

Barbecue Cleaning

Preparing barbecue grills for summer backyard cookouts is tedious and dirty. Grills get coated with burned-on grease and ash, and must be cleaned frequently. Who wouldn't pay to have someone else do it?

Coarse steel wool, degreasers, detergent, and spunk, are all you need to make this job successful. Perfect your technique on Dad's grill, and you'll then know how much to charge.

Basement Cleaning

Basements, attics, and garages have a tendency to gather keepsakes, junk, and dust. The owner will have to decide between the keepsakes and the junk, but dust and dirt is easily identified. You will have to do a lot of lifting, so this is a job for the stronger members of this age group. Attracting customers is simply a matter of going from door-to-door. This job could easily lead into the next three projects.

Salvage Service

I discussed recycling in the previous chapter but limited the discussion to paper, bottles, and cans. As you are cleaning out the basements, attics, and garages, you will discover numerous marketable items that the owner will simply throw away. These items might include steel, aluminum, old car batteries, used tires, old appliances, etc.

You will have to do some scouting around for markets, but they do exist. In the Portland area, I found a battery dealer who paid $5 for batteries (the lead plates are recycled), a tire dealer who paid from $2 to $10 for used tires, a TV repairman who paid $5 to $20 for old TV's, and a used-appliance dealer who paid from $5 to $50 for old stoves, refrigerators, washers and dryers.

Garage Sales

As you clean at these homes, you will see the owners discarding clothes, dishes, games, toys, and many other things that have no value to them, but have marketability. Collect these until you have enough to hold a garage sale, then advertise in the newspaper.

Things which sell well, that your customers will consider discarding, include:

Baby clothes—Babies grow so fast that each outfit is hardly worn. People hang onto them with the intention of giving them to someone else—but never do. New parents are always looking for ways to cut costs, so they are eager buyers.

Baby accessories—I'm astounded by how much paraphernalia it takes to care for a small baby. Much is bought and used for such a brief time that it can be resold at a good price. Cribs, strollers, bassinets, changing tables, and toys are in great demand. Some old items only need a little cleaning and repair to make them into great bargains for some shopper.

Decorating items—Often, very attractive decorating accessories are put into storage because of a color change, new furniture, or because the owner got tired of them. These items can sell well at sales.

Children's games—After the children have grown up, old

Clue and Monopoly games become dust magnets in someone's attic—but hot sellers at garage sales. Toys that have been well-maintained (or reconditioned by you) also sell well.
Clothes—We are a nation of fluctuating fat. Many times perfectly good clothes sit in a closet because the owner's weight is either up or down. Larger sizes often go quite well because people intend to lose that 40 or 50 pounds, so they don't want to spend a lot of money on clothes that they hope will only be temporary.

As you canvass your territory, consider offering to sell things at your garage sale on consignment. People often have several items too good to throw away, but not enough to justify a sale or an ad in the paper. If someone offered to include them at a garage sale for a 25 percent commission, I would probably offer them a number of things from my house.

Antiques

I know nothing about antiques, but am always fascinated when I browse the many shops in resort areas. The prices people pay for old things that I would have thrown away are enough to convince me that a few dollars invested in a book on antiques and collectibles would be money well-invested.

Many times, stripping (very hard work!) old furniture can reveal beautiful woodwork that commands a handsome price. Your basement cleaning work could be a valuable asset to this business.

Car Washing

This is a great spur-of-the-moment money-maker—when the sun is out, dirty cars look dirtier! Armed with a bucket, rags, window cleaner, car soap and a chamois, you are ready to canvass your territory for customers. Offer to wash the car for $1.00 to $1.50, using their hose and vacuum. (Cleaning the *insides* of the windows gives you a competitive edge over the exterior-only car washes that so many service stations operate.) Vacuum the interior for 75 cents to $1.50 (depending on car size). This would produce a maximum charge of $3.00, which is $1.00 below the 1979 full service rates on the West Coast. If you'd like to add a touch of "class" to your job, clean the tire sidewalls with household spray cleaner, and apply dressing to vinyl roofs and dashboards! As I noted in chapter five, this job goes much faster with two people, so it is a great project for siblings to do together.

One of the advantages of this job is that it introduces you and your workmanship to many new customers. A quality car washing can lead to many other opportunities for employment, so make sure you leave a card with your name and number with these customers.

Greeting Card Sales

Boys' Life, comic books, and many other publications for young readers advertise opportunities to make spare cash by selling greeting cards door-to-door. Samples are sent on approval or consignment and allow the youngster to use the samples to obtain orders. The cash-in-advance orders allow the salesman to order additional cards as well as to use the profits to pay for his initial kit. Once the samples are paid for, the difference between sales price and cost is to the salesman's profit.

I started in card sales when I was in the fourth grade. Rather than pocketing all the profit, I accumulated operating capital so I could order in larger quantities, thus receiving larger discounts and expanding my profits. This enabled me to have inventory for immediate delivery, which expanded my sales because many people bought a box of all-occasion cards because they had an immediate need for a particular card—but didn't want to wait two to three weeks for an order to arrive.

Eventually, I eliminated the middleman by dealing directly with a wholesaler and buying large enough quantities to obtain discounts of up to 50 percent. At that point, I had more cards than I could market by myself, so I began to pay youngsters in my neighborhood 15 cents to 25 cents for each box they sold (the same commission I received when dealing with my original mail-order supplier). In the eighth grade I reached the pinnacle of my greeting card career—I had seven people working for me at

Christmas time. This job will require much co-operation from Mom to achieve its greatest success. When I sold just a few items and was taking orders, it was easy to ride by bicycle to new territory, but when I began to carry more samples and wanted to make immediate deliveries on certain items, it meant that Mom had to be nearby with the car.

Three times a week, my mother took my salesmen and me out for two hours after school. She normally brought something to read or work on while waiting in the car, but I realize now that there were many other more productive things she could have been doing at home.

I thank God my parents realized that one of the most important things they could do was to teach me that initiative and industry are important virtues.

Card Addressing

If you have good penmanship, or can type well, you can offer another service as you sell cards (or just sell the service without the cards)—addressing Christmas cards.

Our family has been very sporadic in sending cards because of the time involved in addressing them. If some enterprising youngster (or even oldster) offered to address and stamp my envelopes for five cents each, he would have a customer.

I timed myself and found that I could easily address 80 to 100 envelopes an hour, which would mean that I could earn a minimum of four dollars an hour. This could easily expand into other services, like updating the Christmas list, organizing it on index cards for easier reference, helping to wrap and ship gifts, etc.

Normally, people have their names imprinted on their cards, but if not, make sure the cards are signed before you seal the envelopes. In fact, you might leave the envelopes unsealed and allow the senders the option of a short note on some of the cards. Since you have saved them all the time in addressing their cards, many customers will feel free to add a little personal touch.

Christmas Decorations

The matter of Christmas decorations lends itself to many potential jobs. Here are some:

Lights—Around Thanksgiving pass out flyers announcing your availability to help install and remove exterior Christmas lights. Having done such decorating myself, I have learned that though it is a two-man job, there are fewer arguments when the two workers are unrelated.

Wreaths—While fir boughs are the traditional material for wreaths, I have seen attractive wreaths around the country made of local materials, such as cactus, eucalyptus, pods, pineapples, cones, etc. Depending on your location, much material can be found outdoors at no cost. A minimal investment in ribbons, balls, bells, and wire can aid you in creating $5.00 to $9.95 (sounds much cheaper than $10.00) wreaths. Make several samples and take orders, but have a couple in reserve for people who need immediate delivery.

Trees—While most families decorate their trees together, some would gladly pay to have it done. (They might even commission you to buy, set up, decorate, take down and dispose of the tree.) If you are skilled at hanging tinsel, you may find some willing customers. (Hanging those strands one-by-one is such a tedious job—one of the reasons I favor flocked trees.)

Candles—Candles are in great demand at Christmastime, and you can make money selling those you made yourself (see "Candle making"), or attractive ones you have purchased through a wholesaler. As in any direct sales effort, recognize that every house does not generate a sale.

Assuming the candles you sell for $7.95 cost you $4.00, average sales of only one candle an hour will earn you $3.95, which is more than you would earn in most jobs available to young teens.

Cones—If you live near an area where large cones can be collected (pine cones are especially good), you can combine chemistry with nature and make colored pine cones. By soaking the cones in chemicals, you can create fireplace "decorations" that burn with various colored flames—a blue flame comes from copper sulfate, yellow comes from table salt, etc.

Large sugar pine cones sell as table decorations, and I

have seen attractive "Christmas tree" centerpieces made from decorated cones. If thistles grow in your area, spray paint them red, attach a little cotton beard and black cardboard shoes, and you have a cute Santa Claus.

Giftwrapping—Most major stores provide wrapping service during the Christmas season, but often a local shopping mall will have several stores that do not. Obtain permission from one of the merchants to set up a table to operate a wrapping service. You will have to maintain regular hours for the store to allow you this, so it might be best for you and some friends to establish a partnership.

Provide several inexpensive papers and ribbons, but display several samples of "custom" packages on your table. Ask your customers if they prefer the regular or custom wrapping.

Pricing this service can be done in various ways. One method is to have a price list for various size packages and grades of materials. It would be good to have extra boxes for sale, too.

A method that we found quite effective was asking for a voluntary donation for the regular wrap and ribbon (buying in large rolls kept our cost around 15 cents per normal package—wrapping paper is very cheap right after Christmas) and posting prices for the custom wrap. We found that most people gave us from one-third to one-half of our custom price, so gauge your custom prices accordingly.

In this job you may learn about competition, because many clubs and organizations operate wrapping centers during the holidays; it is not unusual to see several tables in the same mall. If another table nearby is underselling you, you must decide how to react. (This is also true in any job you do—from mowing lawns and washing cars to providing pet services; what your competition charges will affect you.)

You can respond to competition in one of three ways. First, you can ignore it, and simply smile when people tell you about lower prices elsewhere. Second, you can meet or beat it by lowering your price. Third, you can acknowledge their price and use it to show the quality difference that makes your product or service worth the extra:

"Yes, we know what they are charging and feel that they are doing a fine job, but because we use a heavier paper, we need to
charge a little extra."

Shoveling Snow

When the snow starts falling, your neighborhood becomes a
marketplace! Driveways often must be shovelled before a car can
be garaged—and Dad is normally off at work with that car. As
soon as school dismisses, hit the streets with your shovel and
offer your services from door-to-door. Pricing should be from
$2.00 to $3.00 per hour.

Once you have done a driveway, convince the owner to contract with you for shoveling his driveway every time it snows. Before my boys were old enough, I would have gladly paid a reliable
person $4.00 so that I could come home after a new snowfall and
be able to drive into my garage without a care—it's frustrating
to battle snowy roads and then have to get out and shovel the
drive before I go in and relax.

Wood Stacking

While in Portland, Oregon, I once checked the local paper
and noticed a large price difference between suppliers for cords of
wood cut and delivered to the door—but almost all of them
charged $10.00 a cord for stacking. Depending on how far the
wood has to be carried, it takes between 20 to 45 minutes to stack
a cord of wood.

Contact a number of wood sellers advertising in the paper
and offer to stack their deliveries for $7.50 a cord. (A wood cutter
doesn't want to take time to stack, because he can earn more cutting and delivering.) This job almost always works best with two
people, and even counting travel time will net each of you $4.00,
or better, an hour.

Worm Digging

Various government agencies, during the past year, have given much attention to worms—actually, not to the worms themselves, but to the selling of large worm farms. What I suggest here is not a massive worm business, though, but simply providing a service to fishermen in your area.

One of our neighbors filled an old bathtub with compost and grew worms in it. His son managed the worms and could always be counted on to have a fresh supply when we wanted to go fishing. He charged about half the store price, so we were steady customers. At the corner of our street was his only advertisement—a sign with an arrow:

Fish Filleting

Many times, when returning from deep-sea fishing, I have seen youngsters at the dock offering to clean and fillet fish. You will have to check in your area to see what fee can be charged, because I have never used such services (I've never caught anything). Make sure you've mastered your fillet knife before hiring out.

Game Bird Cleaning

Hunting is exciting, plucking feathers is a drag! Place posters at sporting goods stores, hunt clubs, and rifle ranges, offering your service. Do a good job for your first few customers—you will have many referrals. Pricing will vary according to the area, but any job should net you at least $1.50 an hour.

Fresh Eggs

If you live in a rural area, you have different opportunities to make money. Raising chickens and selling their eggs is very profitable. How much money you make on this project will depend on how many chickens you have and how much time you devote to the business.

Establishing customers is no problem; most people like fresh eggs, especially at a lower price. Once you have regular customers, however, you will need to manage your flock carefully because people will count on you for a regular supply. It is best if your customers come to you, but if you must deliver, try to combine the trips; better yet, have other products and services available to your egg customers.

Livestock Raising

My brother joined the Future Farmers of America (FFA) during his high school years, and raised a variety of livestock for profit. Organizations such as 4-H and FFA help many young people in rural areas (sometimes in cities, too) to learn responsibility and business management, while raising livestock or cash crops for profit. Check with one of these organizations in your area and see what opportunities are available if you're interested.

Barbed Wire Plaques

While giving a seminar in DeKalb, Illinois, I discovered that barbed wire was first invented in this town. Until that time, I assumed barbed wire was barbed wire, but I now know there are over 400 *different* kinds of this jagged stuff that snags your clothes during country outings.

I brought home a souvenir from DeKalb that could easily be a money-maker for you. Collect five varieties of wire (almost every farmer has some rolls of old wire sitting behind a shed, and he'd be glad to have you take some); cut the wire into three or four-inch sections, with a barb in each section. Mount the pieces on a five-by-ten inch board covered with burlap.

Invest in a barbed wire "encyclopedia" so you can label each type of wire with its proper name, and you will create $4.95 wall plaques! These plaques sell well at craft shops and tourist shops.

Square Nails

Watch for older homes and buildings being torn down in your

neighborhood. Such buildings may have been constructed with square nails that can be used creatively to make money.

I have seen a very attractive wall plaque that displayed seven or eight different sizes of these old nails. I wear a cross that was made by brazing several square nails together. I have even seen square nails being sold for 5 cents to 25 cents each. Methods of marketing are limited only by your imagination.

9

Junior High to Exhaustion
(Usually College)

By the time your child is a teenager, he will feel that he is ready to handle most areas of his life and will want to make his own decisions, including money. If you have properly trained your child, he will have already learned how to encounter new areas of responsibility that will be discussed in this chapter.

However, if your child is at this age and you have never even thought of giving financial training until now, don't despair. Let me show you how to "start from scratch" with your teenager.

"Starting Over"

During my seminars, I often discuss the issue of teaching children to save on expenses. Inevitably, a conversation like the following ensues:

"That's really great, the way you describe it; obviously your children share your same thrift. But my daughter wouldn't be seen dead in any tennis shoes but Nike" (the same could apply to other name brand shoes, clothing, etc.).

"I'm beginning to appreciate that," was my most recent reply, "because both my boys are showing more concern with what everybody else is wearing. If they choose, for instance, to spend $25 on one shirt, that's their decision. Of course, that would wipe out their whole year's budgets for shirts, but if they want to wear the same shirt every day for a year, that's their prerogative!

"They may earn as much extra money as they desire and spend it for what they want, but I'm not responsible for making them the best dressed in their school."

"That's easy for you," was the incredulous reply. "You've been teaching your kids all along. We've always just given them what they needed, so how can we suddenly give them responsibility for what we've always provided? Won't they resent it?"

"Why," I probed, "do you want to change things now?"

"Because they have to learn that money doesn't grow on trees."

That is *precisely* what I attempt to convey to parents about their children. When parents finally realize that they have failed to train their children in a critical aspect of life—financial management—they also acknowledge that they don't know how to start. Well, here's how.

First, *commit yourself to openness with your child.* One of the worst mistakes you can make is to hide your income and financial condition from your child. Your child will *learn* by observing how you handle your money—whether you succeed or fail.

Openness is also needed in assessing your own attitude. If your child is overly conscious of brand names in clothing, it is often a reflection of *your* attitude. Maybe you wouldn't pay $35 for a pair of tennis shoes, but how much do you pay for your golf sweaters? If you pay $35 for tennis shoes, don't complain that your child wants to spend the same for his. If you want to teach him discretion and restraint in spending, then *you* must set the example.

Second, *have a conference with your spouse to determine your objectives.* If you are a single parent, find someone in your church who is doing a good job training his children and confer with him. Define the problems and what you can do about them. It is best to write them out and to outline the possible solutions.

If the problem is that your child is continually asking for money, the solution is to help him establish a regular budget. If the problem is that he doesn't take good care of his bicycle, make a policy that he must pay for all repairs out of extra earnings.

Third, *have a conference with the child.* This is where openness must begin; you may have to start by asking his forgiveness because you have not properly trained him to handle money. Explain to him that two-thirds of all divorces have a root problem relating to money, and that you desire to give him all the necessary tools needed to handle his money according to God's principles.

Show him your budget and what you are doing to be a good steward, and then ask him what he would consider an adequate monthly amount for him to manage. Most teens I've talked with wouldn't resent this; they are eager to have their own money to manage as they see fit.

When you and your teenager work out his budget for personal care and clothing items, agree together that he has to earn any extra money necessary to purchase the more expensive items he might prefer. Even if you can easily afford to pay all such costs, you will benefit your teen the most by allowing him to earn the extra things—he'll appreciate them much more.

During this conference, formulate a written budget and agree on the frequency of payment. With older teens, semimonthly or monthly payments are best for aiding them to develop discipline.

Your child must also learn the discipline of record-keeping. The forms in chapter nine are comprehensive and help to develop all the skills needed to handle money. Chances are, your teen will expect *you* to use the same discipline in your life. Bethany Fellowship publishes a home budget system which I created called, *Financial Planning Guide for Your Money Matters.* This guide is available through your local Christian bookstore, or send $6.75 to: Your Money Matters, Box 82, Gresham, Oregon 97030. (For an additional $4, instructions on cassette tape are available.)

I don't pretend that making your teen a good manager will be an easy, overnight task. You have already spent several years "teaching" him by example; it will take time and effort to reverse the effects of past mistakes, both in *your* habits and in his responses to your new example. Some of you, at this point, are asking this: "We have plenty of money; why should we have to endure all that time and hassle looking for 'specials'? After all, 'time is money' and it seems that I'll have to waste a lot of time attempting to save a few dollars. Anyway, I've gone after sale items before and the stores never have anything worthwhile—that's the reason they have the items on sale, because all the good merchandise is gone."

The answer to this objection is the word STEWARDSHIP. A steward is someone who manages another's property; *you* are managing a portion of *God's* property. Our family approaches this matter seriously, and last year gave over 30 percent of our income to God's work and people.

One reason we were able to do this is that we purchased over $2,000 in clothing, furniture and household goods for under $400. Though we purchased some used items, much was brand new merchandise "on sale"—in the exact size and color needed. I *expect* my God to provide that type of bargain so that I can free more of His money for "Kingdom work" (one purchase was a $67.50 sport coat for $10.87). Our savings would have been greater except for the purchase of a $350 hide-a-bed for $189.

We did not spend a lot of time doing this shopping. As a matter of fact, we had less time to spend this last year because of our involvement in Youth With A Mission. God provided our needs very rapidly with comparatively little shopping time invested. It was almost as if we would state a need and God would instantly provide.

Our family learned much about God's character and power this past year because we didn't have the income to just go out and buy. I feel every Christian family should attempt this kind of venture sometime.

Bank Accounts

Many savings and loans, and credit unions, have more convenient business hours than banks, and can be excellent places to start your child's account. Our three oldest children have accounts in their names *only* at a local savings and loan. They are paid monthly and are expected to deposit that money into their accounts, and keep track of it in their records. As they need things, they withdraw from their accounts to pay for necessary items.

With each deposit and withdrawal they receive a transaction slip on which they record what the money is for (much the same way you record information in a check register). At the end of each month, we review their expenditures and make sure everything has been recorded properly.

The record-keeping that my children are required to do for their monthly reports is excellent training, and is preparing them for the day when they open their own checking accounts. Since I am giving them freedom to manage their savings accounts, I presume they will develop the necessary discipline and skills to handle checking accounts.

I also recommend that children manage the *family* accounts for a period of time. As each of our children enters high school, he is given the responsibility of writing all the family checks during bill-paying time (I still sign them, but the kids do all the preparation and bookkeeping). The results will be obvious: I was thrilled one day to hear our oldest son reply to a sibling's request to eat out, "Are you kidding? With all the money we just spent on our vacation, we'd almost need to float a loan for entertainment this month." (I was so tickled by that reaction that I took everybody out to dinner, using *my allowance money* rather than the entertainment/vacation funds.)

If you are just beginning to teach your child money management, work very closely with him when he first opens his savings and/or checking account. Attempting to withdraw nonexistent funds from a savings account is embarrassing. Overdrawing a checking account results in costly overdraft and returned-check charges. Bad checks also can mar one's credit record—sometimes important when applying for a job.

Teen Credit Cards

I have one word of advice about teens and credit cards: DON'T! Magazine articles will tell you that credit cards are a must in today's society, so you must train your child how to handle them. Many stores encourage this by issuing credit cards for high-schoolers (with parental permission, but not with the parents' guarantee) to help them develop the credit-card habit.

Let me challenge some credit-card myths:

1. *You must have credit cards to cash checks.* I have *no* credit cards, yet I cash checks all over the world. What I have are check I.D. and check guarantee cards. Most banks issue guarantee cards, and many chain stores provide I.D. cards that enable one to write checks without a credit card.

2. *You must have credit cards when you travel.* I travel worldwide without credit cards. I rent cars, check into hotels and motels, and weather emergencies—all without credit cards. Also, I carry very little cash on trips, since I procure free traveler's checks from my local savings and loan (or credit union or bank).

Cash deposits at car agencies and hotels replace the credit cards. This cash arrangement is normally prearranged, but can be done on-the-spot as well.

You may wonder, what about an emergency that requires more than my traveler's checks could cover? Isn't a bank card essential to meet this eventuality? "But my God will supply all my needs according to my VISA card"—is that what Scripture teaches? Let me relate an example from my travels. A couple of years ago, I was stranded in Fort Wayne, Indiana, en route to one of my seminars in Chicago. My flight was cancelled, due to a snowstorm, and a commercial flight was unavailable until after 4:00 p.m. the following day. The seminar began the next morning, so this was unacceptable.

I approached the Piper dealer at the airport to arrange a private charter; the cost would be $292. I was not elated about the expense, but it seemed to be the only way I could reach Chicago in time for the seminar.

I didn't have enough cash or traveler's checks with me, so I explained that the dealer would have to bill me.

"We can just put it on your Master Charge or VISA card," he suggested.

"I don't carry those cards," I replied, "but, I would be happy to pay the long-distance charge if you'll call my bank and verify that I can and will pay it."

He decided this would be too much trouble, so he asked

me if I could fly to Chicago from Columbus, Ohio. A call to the airline confirmed space, and he offered me a ride with a charter—already paid for—to Columbus, and connect to Chicago from there (an alternative that he would not have offered had I been carrying credit cards to meet this emergency).

"Give the pilot an extra $20 for Christmas," he said, "and we'll call it even!" So for $20, not $292, I flew to Columbus—and missed my plane by five minutes!

Now what? I had never been to Columbus in my life, and had no acquaintances there. I was also down to my last $25, so I couldn't afford a $38 room at the Holiday Inn. If ever a credit card could have been used for an emergency, this was the time!

I went to a phone booth, pulled out the Yellow Pages, and looked up my "family"—under the heading, "CHURCHES." I made a telephone call, and twenty minutes later, a brother in Christ picked me up, brought me to his home, fed me, provided a bed, woke me in the morning, fed me breakfast, and returned me to the airport. I arrived at Chicago in time for my seminar.

I met two tremendous members of the family of God that night, and, quite frankly, would have never thought to call them if I had carried "plastic money" in my pocket. I strongly oppose "free loading," but when a Christian has a genuine emergency, what better help could he possibly find than fellow-members of the Body of Christ?

3. *You must establish credit to buy a house.* This is not true. A house is a *collateral* loan, not a *credit* loan. If you earn sufficient income to justify the monthly installment, and can present the down payment, you will probably be able to qualify for a home loan. You need not have bought anything on "time" to obtain a home loan.

In fact, many lenders are very favorable toward a couple that have disciplined themselves to forego the pleasures of "now," to accumulate a down payment for a home. Such a couple is not likely to immediately buy furniture and household goods on credit. I have counseled too many young marrieds who are being forced to sell their "dream homes" to pay for the extras that they "just had to have" when they moved in.

Here's an idea for a good "field trip" to help your child understand the consequences of wrong use of credit cards. In over 200 cities in the United States, there are nonprofit corporations called Consumer Credit Counsellors. Go with your child to the CCC office in your area and ask the manager to tell about the couples they are dealing with, and the credit traps on which they have become entangled. We vaccinate against measles—such a trip would be a good vaccination against unwise use of credit!

Wedding Bells

Not my babies! They're too young! That's my reaction to the subject of marriage. But, I know that many young people will marry right out of high school, or in their first years of college.

Jim Underwood, president of the National Institute of Christian Financial Planning, a group that conducts seminars and counsels couples about money management, identifies the number one problem faced by most couples as *failure to identify goals.* Help your child adopt goals that include financial freedom. Underwood states that being financially free means living without any of the following symptoms of personal financial problems:

1. You are preoccupied with thoughts of money, at the expense of thoughts about God.
2. You don't give what you feel God wants you to give.
3. You are not at peace to live on what God has provided.
4. You argue within your family about money matters.
5. You can't or don't pay credit cards in full each month.
6. You need or have considered a consolidation loan.
7. You receive notices of past-due accounts.
8. You charge items because you can't pay cash.
9. You use spending as emotional therapy.
10. You spend impulsively.
11. You invade savings to meet current expenses.
12. Your net worth does not increase annually.

13. You "just can't save."
14. You are underinsured.
15. "You wish you had a plan for spending and saving and are frustrated because you don't."*

Establishing and pursuing proper financial goals will forestall tremendous anguish in future years. George Fooshee quips, "Not a single couple has ever told me, 'Well, we did it. By our deliberate overspending, we've reached our three-year goal of owing $10,000. Our frequent arguments over money and the financial pressures we feel are just what we planned. The thrill we feel as we look forward to paying off these debts is the highlight of our marriage.' "*

The Success Factor

Since we have just discussed planning and setting goals, let's determine what your child should have learned about money and money management by the time he graduates from high school.

1. *He has learned how to manage money.* Rather than simply handing money to your child when he requests it, devise a plan that allows him to have money that he is responsible to manage. As he gets older, this money management should include a savings account, and eventually, a checking account.

2. *He shares in the household chores.* Even if you are wealthy enough to afford full-time servants, your plan for your child should include teaching him household duties (even cooking, cleaning, and ironing for boys) and requiring these duties to be performed on a regular basis.

3. *He has a written budget.* A budget is a personal financial strategy. Teaching your child early to plan spending and live within that plan develops lifelong habits that will prevent him from sitting in front of my counseling desk. I have *never* met a couple with a *written* spending plan that got into financial trouble.

---

*Both quotations from *You Can Beat the Money Squeeze*, by George and Marjean Fooshee, published by Fleming H. Revell.

4. *He keeps proper records.* A Harvard Business School study showed that 100 percent of the small businesses surveyed, that experienced financial difficulties, showed poor record-keeping. The study also noted that 100 percent of the businesses surveyed, which were thriving, exhibited clear and informative records. Good records are essential to financial success and freedom.

5. *He has a savings account and understands the place of insurance in planning for future goals.* To help prepare me for the future, Dad obtained a small insurance policy in my name when I was 17. This policy had a guaranteed convertability feature that has enabled me to increase my coverage as needed. Our agreement was that Dad would pay the premium on the policy until I graduated from college, or was employed full time, or was married—whichever came first. In establishing the savings account and insurance package, you need to teach your child the balance between providing for oneself and trusting in God. If one's insurance and savings ever replace trust in God to meet life's needs, then one has moved away from the position of faith that God desires.

6. *He has earned extra money with jobs outside the home.* No matter how well God has provided for you, your child needs to learn how to work. The only way I know for a child to discover the problems of working for a boss who is not his parent is to help him get a job outside the home.

I have already shown that I think self-employment is the best type of job because it requires self-motivation and discipline. Once a child learns these valuable lessons, he will be able to work for another person much more productively.

7. *He has participated in the family's financial planning.* In our complex society, it is essential that your child learns to balance income against expenses. It is one matter to manage his own clothing and personal-care budget; it is quite another thing to manage an entire household.

He should learn to sit down with the family and discuss goals, rather than argue over money. Such discussions will teach him that he must make choices between pleasures of *now* and plans for the *future*. As part of this family participation, make sure your child manages the family budget for a period of at least six months.

8. *He has learned contentment and good shopping habits from your example.* Albert Schweitzer once said, "There are only three ways to teach a child: the first is by example, the second is by example, the third is by example." Your actions are going to speak much louder than your words, so if you aren't willing to be your own best pupil, don't even bother trying to teach your child about money. By exhibiting to your child contentment and good shopping habits, you will be obeying God's guidelines for your own life.

9. *He has learned to honor the Lord by paying his tithes.* What did J. C. Penney, John D. Rockefeller, and Walt Disney have in common besides riches and success? Each was taught early in life, and practiced until his death, the principle of tithing. I think their example is a good one!

A Note About Taxes

As your child enters his teenage years, his money-making projects may become highly profitable, as in the cases of some examples I will note.

As long as your child is classified a dependent, the government allows him to earn several hundred dollars, tax free.

However, if his income rises into a taxable bracket, make sure he fulfills his obligations to the Internal Revenue Service, as well as to state and local governments. Since he will be self-employed, he will need to file a Schedule C, and probably an SE, in addition to the usual Form 1040.

Tax time, of course, is when clear, accurate records are invaluable.

JOBS

Many jobs described in the previous chapter are also applicable to the teenager; so, after you read this section, you may want to review chapter eight. The jobs in this section will normally require more maturity, both physically and emotionally, and some will require a car to achieve full income potential.

Newspaper Clipping Service

Often when a baby is born the new parents will enter a birth announcement in the local paper. If they are like us, they subsequently scour the neighborhood to find extra copies for the baby book and relatives.

I remember the time when my employer had my promotion announced in the newspaper. I spent a small fortune purchasing newspapers to send to my relatives. (I'm not really sure that my relatives wanted them, but I certainly wanted to send them copies!)

Such news items have marketing potential. Approach the manager of an appropriate business (insurance agency, jeweler, furniture store, diaper service, etc.) and contract to search through local newspapers for applicable news items, and send a copy to the person featured. Have him print up a card to accompany the clipping, that says,

> Hello! I was going through the paper and saw this good news about you. If you're like me, you can never find enough copies for your use, so I clipped this one out for you. Congratulations!
> John J. Diamond
> Diamond and Son Jewelers

You can usually confirm the person's address by checking the telephone directory (often, the article contains the address), so your duties would include clipping the article, mailing it, and providing your customer with a list of persons receiving clippings and a description of each clipping. Your customer will thus have a list of potential customers to call on; and he has already established goodwill through your clipping service! Newspaper clippings from a merchant might include a coupon offering a discount or free gift. I don't know of many merchants that use this public relations tactic, so you may have to "sell" the idea. Convince the merchant to give you a one-month trial with a definite budget.

Before you start such a venture, study your local papers for a week and estimate how many "good news" articles might be mailed during that period. You may also find that you need to charge on a variable scale, depending on the type of article involved—50 cents for birth announcements (for a diaper service or baby store) and engagement and wedding announcements (for a jeweler or furniture store); 75 cents for business section announcements (for insurance agencies and banks); $1.00 for general news stories (these normally will require the most research to find the right name and address and could be used by department stores).

Mailing Service

This service could be salable to businesses, churches, and clubs. Many of these organizations send out regular mailings, which entail updating the mailing lists, addressing and stuffing envelopes, sorting, and delivering to the post office. Set a fee competitive with commercial mailing companies.

Lately, I have noticed that a number of businesses are mailing out hand-addressed advertising material. The reasoning? People tend to throw away obvious "junk mail" without even opening it. Mail that is hand-addressed, however, has a "personal" touch that is much more appealing.

If you have good handwriting, this can be a money-maker. Charges will vary, depending on what your competition charges. Call a local mailing service and ask for their prices. In our area, I could charge 10 cents per letter plus 25 cents for each mailing list change. This would put me below local competition, but I would have to convince the buyer of the benefits of hand-addressed envelopes (if you have bad handwriting, but are a good typist, you could probably sell the service and benefits of individually typed addresses). At 10 cents per letter, I could easily clear $5.00 an hour—much better than wages at the local burger shop.

Menu Planning

Working mothers would be obvious customers for this service. Scan the midweek grocery specials to find the best bargains for that weekend. Using these specials, prepare a week's evening menus with two alternate meals (nine meals). Include recipes, and list at least two meals that can be pre-mixed and stored for "emergency" cooking. Your menu plan would give the list of ingredients that are on sale, and where.

This service has two selling points. First, the working mother often spends more money on food because she buys a lot of pre-pared, convenience foods. You can provide her a menu plan to help avoid these higher cost meals. Second, a working mother has less time to shop around, so you will do it for her by high-lighting the best food buys of the week in your menu plan.

You should be able to save most working mothers between $35 and $60 a month with this service, so a charge of $4 a week would be reasonable. Mailing, paper and duplicating will cost about 50 cents per customer, so ten customers will net you $35 a week—and valuable lessons in meal-planning and shopping (which could develop into the next project).

Shopping Service

Having taught seminars all over the country and having counseled many couples with working wives, I'm familiar with the tremendous time pressures that working mothers operate under. If you have developed a number of clients for your menu service, it would seem a logical extension to buy those groceries on special and have them available in your home so that your clients can simply stop and purchase the majority of their week's groceries at one place. Probably a good price for this service would be your cost of the groceries plus a mark-up of, say, 10 per-cent.

After you have established such a business you may be able to buy goods at wholesale prices and save your customers even more money. Of course, you could simply make yourself available to do the shopping for your clients according to their shopping lists. This type of service would be priced on a per-trip basis.

Curb Numbering

This job provided me a good deal of money when I was in high school. There is a tremendous potential market in areas where there is a lot of new construction. Our sales approach sounded something like this:

> Have you ever been looking for someone's house and not been able to see the number on the house? If you're like most people we talk to, it happens too often.
>
> We are painting house numbers on the curbs in this area. Our numbers are four inches tall and easily visible at night. We use latex base white paint for the background with black numbers that we guarantee to last at least three years.
>
> Would you like us to paint your numbers while we're here? If we can do them today, it will cost $2.00, but if you call us to do it at a later date, the charge will be $3.00

Actually, with today's spray paints, you would not have to invest in nearly as much paint and equipment as we did. A 4 1/2" x 9" background will handle most house numbers, using four-inch numbers. Stencils for numbers are available from any hardware store. One can each of white and black spray paint with about $8.00 in stencils will put you into business.

Paint the white background with a stencil and allow to dry. Return in about 10 minutes and you can paint in the black numbers. Today you should be able to charge between $3.00 and $5.00 for this.

Mailbox Numbering/Painting

In areas that don't have curbs, but do have mailboxes, you can number mailboxes for profit. If you have artistic ability, you have opportunity to paint these boxes. A friend of ours took a class in tole painting and then decorated her mailbox. This "advertisement" stands in front of her house, and she has since painted several dozen boxes without even leaving her house to find work.

Since you will be going after customers, you should carry a small sample of what your finished product looks like.

Even if you can't do decorative painting, you could make money repainting old, weathered mailboxes.

Wooden Name Plaques

A wooden sign that displays the name MacGREGOR, and

hangs in front of our house, has moved with us four times. The sign was made by routing the letters in the piece of wood, and is mounted with eye hooks. The letters on such signs are often painted, as well.

If you have some woodworking ability, these signs can be sold quite easily to homeowners. I have also seen these signs done with painted lettering, woodburning, metal sculpturing, rocks, shells and other materials. Use your imagination and see if you can come up with some local material that is plentiful and attractive.

Make some samples and then go door-to-door, taking orders.

Wake-Up Service

One of the things I enjoy about traveling is having the hotel desk clerk call me in the morning to make sure I wake up in time. If you live in an area with a lot of apartments, you could provide a wake-up service for $1.00 a week.

For those hard-to-get-up people, you might include a second call, fifteen minutes after the first one, to make sure they are out of bed. Ten to fifteen customers could provide you with an extra $10 to $15 for a half hour's work per day.

Having a partner for this service, or a reliable substitute, is important in case you are ill or out of town.

Coffee and Doughnut Service

When in college, one of the jobs I had to perform, as a pledge in my fraternity, was "wake-up boy." I would prepare coffee and a tray of doughnuts, and take them from room-to-room as I woke up each of the fraternity members.

If you live near several apartment complexes, see if people would desire such a service. Actually, the full service would probably include tea and juice along with the coffee and doughnuts.

Print up brochures and present one to each occupant in the buildings. You must be willing to get up and be consistent with your service. About $6.00 to $10.00 a week would be reasonable for this service. Costs would be about $3.00 per week per customer.

Birthday Cake Service

This idea came to me when I bought a cake for my wife's birthday. Ingredients for a good birthday cake would be only about $3.50; double that costs for your fee and you will still be very competitive. Office buildings in your area are a good potential market—many offices provide a birthday cake for each employee. Design an attractive handout, and give one to each receptionist in a building. College dorms and campus houses are also excellent markets for this product.

Singing Telegrams

If you can sing well, capitalize on this job opportunity. Have a variety of messages and tunes available ("Happy Birthday" to the Hallelujah Chorus, for example). Using a portable cassette recorder, you can even take orchestral accompaniment with you.

Charge $5.00 for "delivery" by phone, and $8.00 if done in person, so you can pay Mom for driving you to most locations within the city limits. For messages outside the city limits, charge extra.

Your advertisement should invite potential customers to call you for a free "sample." This means you must practice several anniversary, birthday, valentine, etc., messages but this should gain you many customers. You might even hire friends to write lyrics for familiar tunes.

If any of you decides to provide this service in my city, please let me know; I will use you often for in-person singing gifts to my friends! Only five messages a week will net you $25. Happy singing!

Sewing Service

If you like to sew, you can use this money-maker throughout your life. One woman in our church earns between $250 and $300 per month with her sewing service. She sews four hours each day, four days a week, and has two fitting sessions in addition to that. She earns close to $5.00 per hour, and is able to work at home with no transportation or baby-sitting costs.

One of the best ways for you to start your business is by offering a repair service. Many people just don't have time to match and sew on buttons, rehem dresses, and repair tears.

Advertise at laundromats in your area—on their bulletin boards. Check, too, with local laundries and dry cleaners about repair work for them. Find out what others are charging and make your fees competitive.

Typing Service

When I had my CPA practice, I was continually looking for reliable typing help. I had a secretary, but sometimes there would be more than she could handle, so we would hire outside assistance. Normally, we would even take the typing to the person's home, so this could be a money-earner even if you don't have transportation.

Similar to the practice of sending hand-addressed mail, many businesses want to send duplicated letters to their clients, but want them to look individually typed. Short congratulatory notes on birthdays and anniversaries would be excellent for a local insurance agent or jewelry store to send out.

Yard Service

If you have been mowing lawns, you might be able to market a whole range of services to your lawn customers. In the fall, contract to prepare for winter by insulating or shutting off faucets, cleaning and storing barbecue gear, trimming plants, and digging up flower bulbs. In the spring, you could clean up winter damage, weed flower beds, trim shrubbery, clean and put out patio furniture, etc. Charge an appropriate hourly fee.

Storm Cleanup

While writing this portion of the book, I was in Portland, Oregon, during one of the worst ice storms that I've seen there. In the east section of town, almost every yard was littered with broken tree limbs and other debris as a result of the heavy ice.

Several weeks later, many yards still had not been cleaned up. Most of those yards were not cleaned up because the owners were too busy. Such a situation begs for some youthful enterprise.

The day after such a storm, offer your services door-to-door, and charge customers your usual hourly rate. Keep a list of past customers.

Storm Window Installation

If your area has cold winters, distribute brochures in the early fall, offering to install storm windows. Good marketing always looks to the future, so offer a reduced price for a "package deal" that includes removing the windows in the spring.

The only equipment needed for this job is a tall-enough ladder and good balance. Charge 75 cents to a dollar per window, plus an extra 25 cents for second-story windows.

Gutter Cleaning

Rain gutters accumulate dirt and leaves, and with composition roofs, even small gravel. I never remember the rain gutters on our house until they overflow during the first rain of the season. I can testify that cleaning rain gutters during a downpour is a horrible job!

If someone had come a few days earlier and offered to clean my gutters for a reasonable price, he would have had the job. All you need are a ladder, a stiff brush, and a bucket. I think that you could go onto one block and get quite a few customers.

Pool Service

If you live in the sun belt, you could develop a year-round business cleaning backyard swimming pools. We owned a pool when our children were smaller, and I remember spending most of my time cleaning the pool, leaving little time to enjoy it myself.

If you have your own pool, you probably know how to test the water, add chemicals, vacuum the pool and backwash the filter. If you don't, offer to take care of a neighbor's pool for two weeks free if he will instruct you. After those two weeks, your instructor could very well become your first customer!

Since most pool owners already own equipment and chemicals, you will not have to invest any money to start this service. Check what professional pool services are charging in your area and price your work competitively. In our area, $8 a week for two visits, or $5 for one, would be well below the professional rate, and should get you a number of jobs.

Clean on Tuesdays and Saturdays, and stagger the one-a-week clients, or bunch them into Saturday. Four regular customers and two once-a-week customers would add $42 a week to your income, for about eight hours of work.

Photography

As you enter high school, you will discover many areas where photography can pay off. I remember the Sadie Hawkins Day events at my school, and the photos we bought of mock weddings with Marryin' Sam. With the inexpensive instant cameras now available, you could make yourself available for this type of event.

As you improve your skills and equipment, you will find that action photos and candid shots can be sold to the school newspaper and yearbook, as well as to the general student body. (I remember one photo that was a gold mine for our school photographer—he captured the touchdown that won our school the division title, and marketed enlargements through the student store.)

Advertise your availability to take pictures at birthday parties. I always seem to get so busy that I miss some of the important shots at our children's parties. If someone were available to shoot a roll of film at cost, plus $4 to $5, I believe I would be a customer. Try it and see how it works!

Key Chain Photos

The birth of our fourth child was followed by the inevitable hospital photos. In the packet of photographs was an interesting addition—a key chain with a photo of Gordon. It was an optional gift, costing $2.50 or $3.00.

I checked this out and discovered that these key chains can be ordered in fairly minimal quantities for about 15 cents each; slide-viewer chains were available for about 25 cents. At those prices you could shoot action and humorous photos at athletic and social events, and market the results for a fairly healthy profit. I haven't researched this one completely, so if it works well for you, let me know!

Selling Roses

While eating in a nice restaurant one evening, I noticed a nicely dressed young lady come in with a basket of roses. She approached each table and quietly asked the *man* (never the woman first), "Would your lady like a rose this evening?"

In approximately ten minutes, she sold fourteen roses at $1.00 each. Assuming she bought those roses wholesale, she cleared $11.20 during those ten minutes (about $67 per hour!).

This job requires a mature young person, but it certainly offers tremendous possibilities if you live near some nice restaurants that will allow you to come in. (I asked the manager and he noted that the practice was quite good for business. He also indicated that she came in three times during the evening and did very well each time.) You could pocket a good deal of money by making "rounds" through several restaurants in close proximity.

Jewelry Making

I was introduced to this money-earner when my wife took me to a do-it-yourself jewelry shop. I had purchased a pair of earrings for her, only to have them break later that year.

The shop where I bought them was no longer in business, so I thought we would have to throw them away. Not so! We went to the do-it-yourself shop and found all the pieces needed to make the identical earrings for one-fourth the cost of the store-bought pair.

I looked through the various stones, money clips, key chains, tie clips, cuff links, etc., and realized how inexpensively this jewelry could be made. You could create custom jewelry for customers at very competitive prices. Assemble a few samples and take orders.

Market these door-to-door, at women's clubs, or take them into office buildings to show at employee lounge areas.

Candle Making

Sitting on my desk is a beautiful sculptured candle with twirls and twists of multi-colored wax. I watched one being made at Great America and was impressed by how simple the process was that produced a candle worth between $10 and $18. I calculated that the actual material cost less than a dollar, so there is a good profit in each candle.

Investment in equipment can be minimal (discarded metal five-gallon cans could be used to melt the wax), and you can remelt your mistakes as you learn the techniques. I found several books available on making candles, and priced the sculpting tool at under $10.

If you want to start with a less-complicated process, try manufacturing sand candles. Hot wax, with crayons for color, is poured into molds made in sand (I've also seen such molds made with loose loam, bark chips, gravel and other materials). The sand adheres to the exterior, producing a very attractive candle.

Small pieces of driftwood can be placed in the mold for an unusual appearance. Experiment with different designs and let your creativity take off. (I've seen candle/driftwood planters, crosses, wall hangings and other attractive "dust collectors.")

Printing

You've had so much experience making business cards and flyers, if you've tried some of these jobs, so why not open your own print shop? Inexpensive, used printing presses are often advertised in the newspapers. If you need experience, go to your church's printing department or to where your church has its printing done and see if you can help out.

One friend of ours is now putting himself through college with a printing business that he started in the eighth grade. He began by making personalized stationery for his classmates. He was then able to buy an old business-card printer that generated enough profit to purchase his first printing press.

That press gained him almost all his church's printing jobs and much printing from several church members' businesses. He provided a top quality product at a very competitive price. Along the way, he made several costly errors, but learned from them, and will probably graduate from college with a ready-made business to step into (he is majoring in graphic arts, by the way).

Barn-Wood Picture Frames

In any rural area, there are many old, unused buildings. Many times their weathered siding can be used to redecorate homes, but often there are not enough reclaimable pieces to justify the effort of tearing down an old building.

In cases like that, there is usually enough usable wood to make attractive picture frames. I've seen such "barn wood" frames sell at $10 to $50, depending on size.

Go to any art gallery, find the standard canvass sizes, and make a couple of frames as samples to show customers. Galleries are good potential customers, as well as art shops. Once you have made a few sales, word of mouth will bring you other customers.

Shovel Painting

A job title like this one has got to generate interest! Actually, you're not going to paint whole shovels. In fact, you will look for old rusty shovels with broken handles or other damage.

Paint a scene on the blade, braze a picture hanger on the back, and you will have created a $15 work of art. Many of these old shovels can be purchased at garage sales for as little as 25 cents each, so your creative addition will yield a fairly valuable product and a nice profit.

Many crafts stores display this type of work for commissions ranging from 10 percent to 50 percent.

Leather Working

Hand-tooled purses, belts, wallets, wall hangings and many other items can be both fun to make and profitable. Most communities have leather goods stores that sell raw leather products that can be tooled, many times right on the premises with their tools and supervision.

If your community doesn't have such a store, but you'd like to check on prices for raw leather and tools, write to Tandy Products, 1710-1 Tandy Circle, Fort Worth, Texas 76102.

Car Polishing

You will need some practice before you are ready to start charging for this job. Go to a local car wash and ask the workers to teach you a little about waxing. As they wax the cars, see if they'll let you do a little of the work to get the feel of applying the wax and buffing.

After this instruction, offer to do the family car and some neighbors' cars for the cost of materials plus $3 or $4. Once you have gained a little experience, you will be in business.

What you charge will depend on your competition's rates. You probably can charge from $8 for compacts to $20 for full-size cars. The condition of the paint will make a difference. In vicinities that experience high oxidation, you will have to work much harder to produce a good shine.

One of our friends owns a professional shop and tells me that repainted cars can be especially difficult to work with. As you gain experience, you will know how to price your work to compensate for special problems. What you earn will depend on how many cars you are willing to handle in a week. If you polish four or five a week, you could easily clear $60.

Engine Cleaning

A car wash in our area has a steam hose that rents for 50 cents. I've often thought a person could earn a good wage by providing an engine-degreasing service.

Here's the formula. Drive to the steam sprayer, spray degreaser on the engine, let sit for eight to ten minutes, steam off the degreaser, return the car to owner, and collect $10.00. Engine degreaser at a local auto supply store costs about $2.50 per can. Your cost would be $3.00 ($2.50 plus the 50 cents steam charge), so your profit would be $7.00

Car Interior Cleanup

Many areas have exterior-only car washes that do not offer interior cleaning. Many people, like me, have the exterior washed often, intending to clean the interior the next weekend. Unfortunately, that next weekend is spent with other chores, and the car's interior doesn't get done.

Your interior service would include vacuuming (bring your own vacuum and extension cord—old cannister models can be bought at garage sales for $5 to $15), cleaning the windows inside and out, cleaning the upholstery and panels, dusting the dashboard, and emptying all the ashtrays. Advertise your service as a "full service interior cleanup—not just a car wash quickie."

The $1.75 interior cleanup I've received at the local car wash was not nearly as thorough as a cleanup I'd have done myself. If your service is as good as your ad claims, you will be able to charge $2.50 to $4.00 for a job that will take about half an hour. Offer carpet shampooing for an additional $5.00. A can of spray rug cleaner from the grocery store will handle several cars. Lay down paper mats to protect the wet carpet from soiling if the car is used before the carpet dries (cut mats from a big roll of butcher paper).

Car Detailing

Put all three previous car packages together, and you'll have a car-detailing service. When a car dealer takes a car in trade, he has the vehicle detailed before displaying it on the lot for resale. Detailing includes cleaning and painting the engine, polishing the finish, cleaning the interior, shampooing the rugs, cleaning the upholstery, and painting the trunk, to make the car look well-cared-for.

A commercial detailer charges the car dealer $40 to $50 and

the general public is charged $75 for the same service. Little special equipment is needed to do this job and there are many potential customers in any area.

Advertise your service on bulletin boards in laundromats and grocery stores, and pass out flyers. Your lead should be something like this:

> Trading your old car? DON'T—until you've talked to me. I'll clean that car so well that you may just decide to keep it! An expenditure of $20 to $30 could easily increase your car's trade-in value almost $200!

For the $20 to $30 (depending on car size and condition), you will clean the interior, shampoo the carpets, steam clean the motor, and polish the exterior. A friend of ours who manages a local car dealership has informed me that cars that come in clean usually command almost $200 more in trade because cleanliness indicates pride of ownership and good mechanical maintenance.

Car Restoration

If you have mechanical ability and like to do body repair, you could earn an admirable income by restoring wrecked cars. Here's how the son of one of our friends got started.

Tom took mechanical and body repair classes at his high school, so that by the time he was 16, he was a capable mechanic. A neighbor had an older car that had been "totalled" in an accident; because of insurance complications, this car had been sitting in the man's garage for over a year.

Tom examined the car and saw that the engine and major body portions were in excellent condition (the car was one of the early Mustangs and had only 62,000 miles on it). He approached the owner and asked if he could have the car to restore, promising to pay the owner $600 when it was completed and sold. Since this was substantially more than the insurance company was offering, the owner readily agreed.

Three months later, after an expenditure of under $100 for parts and materials, Tom sold a beautiful car for over $2,000 and cleared $1,300. He used the profit to buy several other "totalled" cars from an insurance company (cars that were being junked because the cost to repair them commercially was more than the cost of replacing them) for $200 each.

In one year, he has multiplied that $1,300 into a car that he owns free and clear, plus a $6,000 bank balance. He will graduate from high school this June with close to $10,000 in the bank, and a skill that will easily meet his college expenses.

You fathers that enjoy this type of activity should consider the man who is my spiritual "father." Chaplain Ron has worked side-by-side with each of his three sons as they restored cars in their garage. This time together enabled Ron to not only teach his boys a valuable skill, but also provided many times of sharing and soul-searching together.

As for the boys, this activity furnished each of them with his own car, and ample spending money during his high school years.

Furniture Upholstering

I know nothing about upholstering furniture, but I do know it is costly to have done. Many local school systems offer extension classes in a wide variety of subjects. Annually, our school holds a class in furniture upholstery.

A lady in our church enrolled in this class and used her new knowledge to reupholster her own furniture. She now clears about $300 a month doing custom upholstery in her garage. A high-schooler could just as easily take such a class and begin his own business.

Furniture Repair

In a community we formerly lived in, we had a very active industrial arts department in the high school; the department included a furniture/cabinet making shop. Students in this shop worked with many pieces of old furniture that they restored to mint condition.

Armed with such skills, you could easily earn extra cash by repairing furniture for others, or by buying old pieces at junk stores and garage sales and restoring them. With the antique craze we are seeing today, you could easily find your work creating more demand than you could fill.

Bicycle Repair

My only skill in repairing bicycles is finding the address of the local repair shop! I am no help to my kids at all, but I've noticed that Greg is quite interested in repair and has learned to do almost all his own maintenance.

If you have a "knack" in this area, you could earn money by going door-to-door with your repair service. Make sure you really know what you're doing and take tools and parts with you. There are many repairable bikes sitting in garages and on patios because it's "too much trouble" to load a bike into a car and take it to a repair shop.

Charge for parts plus $5.00 an hour, and you should find yourself with plenty of customers.

Rug Cleaning

Many grocery stores rent carpet cleaners for home use. Volunteer to clean the rugs in your house for the cost of detergent and equipment rental. This will provide you experience with the equipment and various cleaning problems. Do two more houses on this basis (Grandma's and a neighbor's) and you will be ready to launch your business.

Canvass a neighborhood so that you can schedule several jobs in the area, thus realizing the greatest possible use from the rental equipment. Price your work by the square foot of carpet cleaned, plus a per step fee on stairs. Find out what professional cleaners charge in your area and make yourself competitive.

If you do this alone, you will have to require that the carpets be free from any furniture; if you work with someone else, you can price your service a little higher to include moving and replacing the furniture. Once you perfect your technique, you should expect to clear between $40 and $60 per working day.

Upholstery Cleaning

Like rug cleaning, upholstery cleaning is something people *intend* to do but never seem to get around to. Most of these cleaning jobs will be available to you if you simply knock on doors and offer a reasonably priced service to the customer. Upholstery cleaning equipment can be rented from a variety of stores.

Again, cleaning your own furniture, and that of a few neighbors, will gain you the experience necessary to begin this job. Solicit some letters of recommendation from those customers to show potential customers. You will find that furniture and rug cleaning will be a good combination business.

Wall and Paneling Cleaning

Many homes now have paneling that needs to be cleaned and polished if it's to maintain its original beauty. Offer to "restore the luster to your paneling" for the cost of materials plus three dollars an hour.

In addition to paneling, other types of wall materials need periodic cleaning—a chore that many housewives avoid as long as they can. Your ringing their doorbell may remind them they need to do the job—and you may get it.

Waxing and Polishing Floors

Many older homes still have hardwood floors that need to be stripped and rewaxed. As I recall from my youth, this is a tedious and time-consuming job. Remember what I pointed out two chapters ago? The jobs that people don't want to do, and put off, are the ones that offer the greatest income potential. Commercial buffers can be rented and used to give waxed floors a high luster that will gain you many referrals.

Start out by working with the church janitor and helping him to strip, wax, and buff the church floors. Although the job doesn't require a great deal of skill, certain types of wood floors do demand special care.

When in doubt, ask the customer. He will appreciate your honesty. As a homeowner, I would much rather be bothered and tell you that no special care is required than to discover you have ruined my wood floor with your lack of knowledge.

Interior Painting

I once watched a professional painter do a room in about half the time it would have taken me—and he didn't seem to even hurry! I was especially amazed that he could paint the woodwork around windows without getting any paint on the glass. If you can get enough practice to do a clean, drip-free job of painting, you will find more work than you can handle.

You will need to invest in rollers, brushes, drop cloths and ladders. Armed with your equipment, pass out flyers in an area and encourage potential customers to invite you over for a free estimate.

Your fee should be for the labor only; let them buy the paint. Experience will help you to judge how long it will take to do a room. Price your jobs so that you'll earn about $4 to $5 an hour. Your customers will be surprised at how affordable your work is.

Shower and Tub Tile Cleaning

Take a look at your home's shower tile. If it is like that of most homes over five years old, the tile has water spots, and the grout between the tiles has become moldy and grimy. To solve this, you'll need a strong cleaner, a stiff brush (I've used old tooth brushes to clean the grout between our shower tiles), and a lot of elbow grease.

Offer this service in conjunction with other household jobs to make the trip worthwhile, but don't pass up the chance to take a little job. Your willingness and ability to do a good job will gain you other business in the future.

House Refurbishing

Selling a house is like trading a car—the better it looks, the more money it's worth. Often, a home that is on the market lacks "sparkle." The rugs are dirty, some of the walls are smudged and faded, the floors lack a good shine, the bathroom is dingy, the windows need cleaning, and so forth.

One of our friends refurbished an old apartment building to sell as condominium units. He repainted the walls, made minor repairs, shampooed the rugs, and washed the windows. His total expenditure was less than $200 per unit, yet he sold the condominiums for $12,000 more per unit than he had invested.

Go to some real estate agents and convince them to hire you to clean up homes before they're put on the market. The same polish and paint that earned my friend so much extra money will pay dividends to real estate agents. Your service should offer prices for specific types of cleaning as well as a package price.

Kitchen Organizing

A kitchen job that is often put off is the relining of drawers and shelves. This job is often done on impulse, so you might find customers more easily by carrying several patterns of paper with you.

This business could easily expand into a total kitchen reorganization service—not that you would do the work alone, but your presence is often the nudge that a housewife needs to complete the job that she has promised to do for so long. Be prepared to quote an hourly fee for this, after you complete the shelf and drawer lining.

Wood Cutting

As you get older, many other jobs open up. One of these is cutting and splitting firewood. For this job, you will need access to a truck, a chain saw, a splitting maul and, of course, a source of logs. During the winter of 1979-80, wood was being sold for $65 to $90 a cord in Portland, Oregon, depending on the type of wood.

This job is easier and safer with a partner, and can be very profitable. Two people who are willing to work steadily can cut, split, and deliver seven to eight cords of wood a week. Assuming that you average $75 a cord, you stand to clear about $250 a week after expenses.

It's best to have a place in town to store the wood. During the summer months, spend maximum time cutting and splitting your wood so it will be dry by winter. To generate expense money, fill your truck with wood several times a week and park it on a busy corner with a sign displaying your phone number. When a customer calls, offer him a discount if he'll purchase the wood immediately. Make sure you record his name and number for future orders.

During the long summer hours, you and your partner can easily prepare 15 to 20 cords a week, for delivery after the cold weather begins. This seasoned wood will command maximum prices once winter comes—when people can't get into forests to cut their own wood.

Sell only enough wood during the summer to cover expenses and provide some spending money; all the wood that you can inventory for the colder season will increase in value by at least 25 percent. We have one friend who earns an extra $5,000 to $6,000 a year cutting wood in his spare time during the summer, and delivering it during the winter.

Profits from this work are much better than what you might earn at a local gas station.

PART IV

Keeping Abreast of the Facts

10

Write It Down!

Any enterprise is built by wise planning, becomes strong through common sense, and profits wonderfully by keeping abreast of the facts (Prov. 24:3, 4, TLB).

The key to "keeping abreast of the facts" is accurate record-keeping. You help establish *lifetime habits* by training your child to keep daily records.

I've counseled thousands of couples regarding money management. I've never met a couple who had good, accurate records that was in financial difficulty. On the other hand, I've never counseled a couple in trouble that had more than a vague notion of how much they were spending.

You will find that your child enjoys keeping records and that his enjoyment is contagious (you'll start enjoying it). There is much similarity between this system and the one in my adult's *Financial Planning Guide*. As your child matures and acquires full-time employment, he can begin to use the *Financial Planning Guide* with very little adjustment.

Assuming your child presently receives a weekly allowance, here is how to use the forms:

Spending and Saving Plan

In our family, the weekly fixed allowance includes a tithe, Christmas savings, clothing, lunches, grooming and school supplies, and one dollar for "fun." The children earn extra money for

other contributions, extra Christmas money, special clothing
(Greg is a skateboarder, so his pants expenses are higher), half of
church camp, and other extras.

Daily Spending Record

Note that the spaces are large enough to permit recording
both amounts and explanations. For example, "Personal Expenses" for Wednesday could be:

```
haircut ................ $3.00
school paper ........... $1.79
toothpaste ............. $1.39
```
The total from the "Savings" column should be transferred to
the Savings Record. All others are to be transferred to the Spending Record. The amount under "Savings" on the Spending Record is the amount *deposited* into savings for future expenses. The
actual expenditures from savings are recorded in the Savings
Record.

Weekly Spending Record

The "Plan" column entries in this record come from the "Total" column of the Spending and Saving Plan. The "Spent" entries come from the Daily Spending Record (except savings,
which should always be the same as planned).

This form allows you to evaluate your plan's effectiveness.
Most often, the total "Plan" and "Spent" will be the same, but
at times, there will be differences. If differences appear too often,
it is time to examine your self-discipline or the plan.

Savings Record

The "Saved" amounts will correspond with the Weekly
Spending Record. These are regular amounts being saved to
meet planned expenses as they come.

The "Spent" amounts come from the Daily Spending Record.
You will need to make a withdrawal from the savings account to
make these expenditures, so make sure you subtract the spent
amount from the Savings Balance.

WEEKLY SPENDING AND SAVING PLAN

Date

	+Allowance	Extra Earnings	*Total
Tithes & Contributions: Church Sunday School			
Savings: Christmas Clothes Church Camp			
Personal Expenses: Bus Lunches Haircuts Grooming School Supplies			
Fun: Activities Books & mags. Dues (Scouts, etc.) School Annual			
Total			

*To Weekly Spending Record
+This is the fixed amount earned around the house

DAILY SPENDING RECORD

week ended _____

	Tithes and Contributions	Savings	Personal Expenses	Fun
Sunday				
Monday				
Tuesday				
Wednesday				
Thursday				
Friday				
Saturday				
Total				
Notes				

WEEKLY SPENDING RECORD

Totals from Daily Spending Record	WEEK 1 Date		WEEK 2 Date		WEEK 3 Date		WEEK 4 Date	
	Plan	Spent*	Plan	Spent*	Plan	Spent*	Plan	Spent*
Tithes & Contributions:								
Church								
Sunday School								
————								
Savings:								
Christmas								
Clothes								
Church Camp								
————								
Personal Expenses:								
Bus								
Lunches								
Haircuts								
Grooming								
School supplies								
————								
Fun:								
Activities								
Books & mags.								
Dues (Scouts, etc.)								
School annual								
————								
————								
Total								

SAVINGS RECORD

		Christmas	Clothes	Church Camp			Savings Balance
——— Date	Saved Spent						
——— Date	Saved Spent						
——— Date	Saved Spent						
——— Date	Saved Spent						
——— Date	Saved Spent						
——— Date	Saved Spent						
——— Date	Saved Spent						
——— Date	Saved Spent						
——— Date	Saved Spent						
——— Date	Saved Spent						
——— Date	Saved Spent						
——— Date	Saved Spent